# THE GREATER ROMAN
HISTORIANS

# THE GREATER ROMAN HISTORIANS

BY

M. L. W. LAISTNER

UNIVERSITY OF CALIFORNIA PRESS
BERKELEY, LOS ANGELES, LONDON
1971

UNIVERSITY OF CALIFORNIA PRESS
BERKELEY AND LOS ANGELES
CALIFORNIA

UNIVERSITY OF CALIFORNIA PRESS, LTD.
LONDON, ENGLAND

ISBN: 0-520-00688-7

MANUFACTURED IN THE UNITED STATES OF AMERICA

# PREFACE

THAT THE *Roman historians continue to engage the attention of scholars and critics is a proof of their unfailing vitality. Much of what has been written about them in recent years is specialized in its nature; but studies and interpretations of a more general character have not been lacking. Some of these, composed by men thoroughly familiar with the original works and the times in which they were written, have sought to reverse or greatly to modify the estimates of an earlier generation of scholars. There have also been other appraisals. Their authors, without any special acquaintance with antiquity and, as it would seem, with an imperfect knowledge of Greek and Latin, have adopted the simple but fallacious method of applying to the works of the ancient historians contemporary standards of historical inquiry and then passing adverse judgment on them. Thus a fresh evaluation of Sallust, Livy, Tacitus, and Ammianus which as far as possible should judge their writings in the light of the age in which they lived seemed not untimely.*

*The lectures are printed substantially as they were delivered. The main purpose of the notes, which have been kept as brief as possible, is to supply the more important references to the works of the ancient authors or of modern critics. Here and there they have also afforded opportunity for a short discussion of controversial topics. The English renderings from Caesar, Sallust, Livy, and Ammianus are my own. For the quotations from the* History *and* Annals *of Tacitus I have used the version of G. G. Ramsay. Its accuracy, its diction, and the skill with which it reproduces, as far as this can be done at all in another language, the Tacitean manner, entitle it to be numbered among the classic translations in English of an ancient author.*

*I desire to express my sincere thanks to the University of California, which honored me with an invitation to deliver these lectures on the Sather Foundation; and to friends and colleagues in Berkeley whose kindness made my stay there a memorable experience. Professor Harry Caplan of Cornell University with exemplary patience read my manuscript in its entirety and aided me with many valuable criticisms and suggestions. I cannot express my gratitude to him better than by echoing the words of Laelius:* Quid dulcius quam habere quicum omnia audeas sic loqui ut tecum?

M. L. W. LAISTNER

*Cornell University*
*Ithaca, N. Y.*

# CONTENTS

The world exists for the education of each man. There is no age, or state of society, or mode of action in history, to which there is not somewhat corresponding in his life. Everything tends in a wonderful manner to abbreviate itself and yield its own virtue to him. He should see that he can live all history in his own person.

EMERSON

Nicht die Wahrheit, in deren Besitz irgend ein Mensch ist, oder zu sein vermeinet, sondern die aufrichtige Mühe, die er angewandt hat, hinter die Wahrheit zu kommen, macht den Wert des Menschen. Denn nicht durch den Besitz, sondern durch die Nachforschung der Wahrheit erweitern sich seine Kräfte, worin allein seine immer wachsende Vollkommenheit bestehet. Der Besitz macht ruhig, träge, stolz—.

LESSING

## CHAPTER I

# THE HELLENISTIC BACKGROUND

QUINTILIAN in an oft-quoted passage of his educational manual avers that the achievement of the Roman historians can fairly be set side by side with that of their Greek predecessors. Of the four writers with whom these lectures are chiefly concerned, two were already "classics" or standard authorities in Quintilian's day, and one of the two had won the doubtful distinction of becoming the bane of gerund-grinding schoolboys. But even when Sallust began to turn from public life to authorship, Roman historical composition had nearly two centuries of growth and experimentation behind it. The earliest surviving fragments date from a time when Rome was on the point of winning political domination in the western Mediterranean; within little more than fifty years she was to extend it also to the Greek-speaking East. Of her four great historians, Sallust was writing in an era of political revolution. Livy was one of the two stars of the first magnitude in the brilliant constellation that illumined the Augustan age, a disguised and on the whole beneficent autocracy. This absolute rule became rapidly more apparent after Augustus' death and for considerable periods lost much of its beneficence at least in Rome and Italy. In the provinces, as is now generally recognized, prosperity and administrative efficiency, even during the darkest days of Nero or Domitian, did not seriously decline. Tacitus grew up during an era of overt despotism, but he wrote his historical works when the *ancien régime* of Augustus seemed to have been in great measure restored. Finally, Ammianus Marcellinus two and a half centuries later, after an active manhood of military service, turned to historical authorship when the unity and safety of the Empire were alike disintegrating. Barbarian tribes were steadily encroaching on the provincial frontiers, and this process led not only to loss of territories and military insecurity, but inevitably also to the gradual separation of the Eastern from the Western half of the Empire. The length of time from Fabius Pictor to Ammianus is approximately the same as from Matthew Paris to Ranke's middle years; even the shorter span from Sallust to Ammianus is a little longer than from Camden and Holinshed to historians still living. It will therefore be obvious that the four Roman historians show differences of various sorts, due to individual temperament as well as to upbringing and environment. Yet these differences, though not unsubstantial, are less significant than their similarities, a circumstance due to the essential continuity and even unity of Graeco-Roman culture. In Sallust, Livy, and Tacitus, Greek thought has helped to modify the Roman outlook that was their heritage. In Ammianus the process was reversed; the Greek soldier absorbed much of the Roman tradition as it was understood in his day. Clearly, then, any discussion of the Roman historians must be preceded by at least a summary inquiry into the aims and methods of Greek historical writing, particularly during the two centuries after the death of Alexander the Great.

It has become fashionable in recent years, particularly in Germany, to attribute to the Hellenistic historians more originality in their concept of history and their treatment of its subject matter than is warranted by the recorded evidence. In truth, these writers had inherited most of the notions of their craft from the preceding age. Their innovations consisted either in the elaboration of features which earlier writers had treated with relative neglect or in a different distribution of emphasis. The subject matter was taken, as in previous centuries, predominantly from a restricted field, geographically or chronologically, with a decided preference for contemporary or near-contemporary history. Herodotus had essayed a general survey of the Persian Empire or of as much of it as he was able to compass; but his *History,* in the narrower sense of a chronological presentation of military and political events, covered only two decades, with special emphasis on the last three years. Thucydides chose a strictly contemporary theme and Xenophon also in his *Hellenic History* wrote of the events of his own lifetime. Ephorus was an innovator when he proceeded to put together a "universal" history of the Greeks from the beginning of what he regarded as historic Greece to *circa* 340 B.C. He also paid some attention to non-Greek peoples, but only so far as their affairs impinged on those of the Greek city-states. The compilation of chronicles or annals went on side by side with the writing of histories in literary form. This is true of the Hellenistic age also, as we know both from allusions in literature and from occasional mention in inscriptions.[1] The great majority of Hellenistic historians, like their predecessors, favored both restricted and contemporary historical subjects. Amongst these were the exploits of Alexander, the struggle for political control between his successors, or the history of individual monarchies like the Ptolemaic, the Seleucid, or the Attalid. This preoccupation with narrow subjects and the lack of "universal" histories was deplored by Polybius and by Posidonius.[2]

All alike were agreed in their concept of historical writing, as distinct from chronicles, as one form of artistic prose composition. This view of history is as old as Herodotus; and it is not superfluous, in the light of some recent interpretations, to remember that even Thucydides was a child of his age and therefore was deeply affected by the Sophistic movement of his day. In the fourth century Isocrates' influence was not restricted to his special spheres of rhetoric and educational theory and practice; it extended also, though indirectly, to historical composition. His *Evagoras,* the elaboration with which in his political discourses he treats outstanding contemporaries like Timotheus, and his constant use of *exempla* from both the heroic and the strictly historical ages of Greece are all significant. The emphasis on eminent persons is marked also in Xenophon, not merely, as has been wrongly asserted, in the *Anabasis,* but even in his *Hellenic History;* for the second section of that work is demonstrably built up around the personality and achievements of Agesilaos. Equally influential was Isocrates' so-called panhellenism. It may be a matter of dispute what precisely this meant to him and to his contemporaries, nor does it greatly matter for our purpose. The essential point is that it did further a more catholic, less particularistic, approach to both past and present, even though the non-Hellenic neighbors of the Greek city-states continued to receive but little attention. Isocrates' pupils, Ephorus and Theopompus, both undertook the writing of history with this panhellenic outlook, and we have it on the authority of Polybius (v.33.2) that Ephorus' work was, besides, the first attempt to compose a universal history. Isocrates' advocacy, especially in his later years when he despaired of Hellenic unity under the leadership of any Greek state, even of Athens, of Greek unification under the presidency of an absolute ruler like Philip II of Macedon, is also reflected in one of his pupils. Theopompus' most ambitious and most influential work was a history of Greek and Macedonian affairs with Philip himself as the central theme. His historical judgment was far sounder than that of Polybius, who criticized Theopompus for this very thing, but himself displayed a strangely parochial point of view when he remarked (viii.11[13].4): "And yet it would have been far more telling and fair to have included the actions of Philip in the general history of Greece than the history of Greece in that of Philip."

Some other features of Theopompus' historical outlook are significant, although they may also be more open to criticism. He appears to have been the first historian to write under the influence of a particular ethical theory. Even in the relatively few fragments that survive, one is struck by his puritanical approach. Of all Socrates' disciples, Antisthenes the Cynic alone was praised by Theopompus; and his own *saeva indignatio* at contemporary manners and morals, Greek and barbarian, individual and national, was an expression of his sympathy with the Cynic philosophy. For this reason Polybius is again unfair when in the same passage he upbraids Theopompus for his strictures on Philip's private life and intimate companions and conveniently forgets that Theopompus had treated other personages in his book with no less severity. Another and more dubious characteristic of Theopompus, which was often imitated by later writers, was the introduction of legendary and even incredible stories into his *History*. Here, too, Isocratean influence may have been at work, but with a difference. To Isocrates the tales of Heracles or Agamemnon were instructive examples to point a moral or illustrate an argument, the legitimate use of a recognized rhetorical device; but this was a very different thing from the introduction of popular legends into sober history. "Let him," comments a later writer after referring to one of Theopompus' tall stories, "who regards the Chian historian as reliable when he relates this, believe it. For my part I think he is just a smart storyteller ($\delta\epsilon\iota\nu\dot{o}s$ $\mu\nu\theta o\lambda\dot{o}\gamma os$) both in this episode and elsewhere."[3]

Ephorus was a pioneer when he attempted to knit together the history of the whole Greek world from the Return of the Heracleidae down to his own times. Another feature of his work was both important and praiseworthy, though not as influential after his time as one could have wished. He made a serious effort to arrange his *History* according to subjects or broad topics rather than in strict chronological sequence; more precisely, within a general chronological framework he grouped together some of his material, for instance, his account of the Persian wars, according to the subject matter.[4]

The great mass of historical works produced in the two centuries after Alexander's death, with the exception of substantial remains of Polybius, is irretrievably lost. Hence it is difficult, if not impossible, to form a fair estimate of either the best or the worst that was produced, or of the average *History* falling between these two extremes, seeing that we depend on quotations in later authors and on the criticism of his predecessors in the pages of Polybius. The truth is that Polybius' comments are nearly always hostile, so that it is legitimate to wonder whether he is the safe guide for estimating the virtues and faults of earlier historians that he is usually assumed to be. There is at the present time a marked tendency to overrate him, admirable as his book undoubtedly is. His insistent carping at other historians would alone dispose one to question the validity of some of his judgments, even if his own work were invariably above criticism. Yet his bias against the Aetolians is notorious. Aymard has shown how vague and careless Polybius sometimes can be in his technical terminology when he is dealing with the affairs of the Achaean League; while Edson has made out a strong case to prove that in Polybius, as in other extant sources, the whole story of the relations between Philip V and Perseus and the character of Perseus himself have been perverted in the Roman interest.[5]

Of all Polybius' predecessors it is Timaeus who comes in for the harshest censure. He had composed an elaborate history of the Western Greeks and, when an old man, a separate treatise on the wars of Pyrrhus of Epirus. His *History* became a standard work, and much information derived from it is embedded in the later compilation of Diodorus. Unfortunately, far more of the extant fragments come from the later than from the earlier parts of the *History,* in which he had brought together much valuable material about the beginnings of the Greek settlements in Sicily and Italy, and about the Italic peoples and their neighbors. In course of time Roman antiquarians made extensive use of Timaeus. He was proud of, and at times obtruded, his vast erudition, and Polybius amongst other things criticized him for being a cloistered pedant. Yet he had a broader conception of historical writing than his contemporaries. He included in his *History* much geographical and ethnological lore; he also made a determined effort to correlate the various methods used in the Greek city-states of reckoning the course of events and then to employ a single system of chronology that was generally applicable. Less admirable was a marked bias in the political sections of his book and his bitter criticism of others, including Aristotle. If he reported dreams, portents, and other supernatural phenomena in his narrative, he was by no means alone in so doing. We may agree with a recent critic that Timaeus was a deeply religious man, but the critic fails to note that Timaeus had a saving sense of humor. Cicero did not miss this trait, for he writes: "In this connection Timaeus, as he often does, made a witty comment. After relating that the temple of Diana at Ephesus was burnt to the ground on the very night of Alexander's birth, he added that this was in no way surprising, seeing that Diana had been away from home because she wished to be present at Olympias' delivery."[6]

Timaeus, who lived to an advanced old age, marked the transition from the fourth century to the Hellenistic age properly so called; but Cicero is essentially right when he includes him (*De orat.* ii.14.58) with the earlier historians from Herodotus to Theopompus. Of the numerous authors who in the third century B.C. turned to historical composition, only three need detain us, Cleitarchus, Duris, and Phylarchus. The *History of Alexander* by Cleitarchus, as is generally agreed, laid the foundation for that sensational and semilegendary account of the Conqueror's life and achievements which passed to later writers like Curtius, and to some extent to Plutarch. It also inspired the romantic fictions of the pseudo-Callisthenes and so, ultimately, the Alexander romances of the medieval period both in the East and in the

West. Duris of Samos, a pupil of Theophrastus, was a polymath; for, although Cicero calls him (*ad Att.* vi.1.18) *homo in historia diligens,* history was only one of Duris' interests, which included literary criticism, music, and the history of art. Phylarchus' chief work was a history of his own times and was extensively consulted by later writers for the period from 272 to 220 B.C. These three men seem to have had one trait in common, their theory of historical writing. For Duris a connection with the Peripatetics is expressly stated, but this is not so for the other two. Nevertheless, all three are commonly regarded as the leading exponents of the Peripatetic or "tragic" school of historians, a view to which we shall return later. Duris was in conscious opposition to Ephorus and Theopompus, of whom he remarked that "they cut themselves off in the main from the past; for they were devoid of art in their presentation and paid heed only to the narration of events."[7] Polybius introduced a comparison with tragic poets when he censured Phylarchus' detailed descriptions of horrors calculated to work on the feelings of the reader.[8] What these three predecessors of Polybius thought about their craft is, however, only a part of a much wider topic to which we must now briefly turn.

To the Greeks, as to the Romans, a *History,* as distinct from bare chronicles, was always an artistic product; whether it described events long past or those contemporary with the writer's own lifetime was immaterial. In consequence, the composition of a historical work must follow certain rules that had been gradually evolved to govern the writing of any type of artistic prose. The place of rhetoric in the cultural life of classical and postclassical Greece has frequently been stressed; it has also often been misunderstood. The formulation and elaboration step by step of principles to which a prose composition must conform was in essence no different from the growth of an artistic canon in the plastic arts or the evolution of various recognized forms of poetic composition. The civic life of the Greek states, involving, at least in democratic cities like Athens, personal participation in the conduct of affairs and in the courts of law, determined the type of prose to which theorists primarily turned their attention. Thus the study of oratory—forensic, deliberative, and epideictic,—which reached its highest development in Demosthenes and Isocrates, inevitably exerted a profound influence on other kinds of prose writing. Of these history was one. The influence of the early Sophists is clearly observable already in Thucydides, not merely in the speeches but in the purely narrative portions of his *History*. Yet in the fifth century formal rhetoric was still in its infancy; it was the fourth which saw not only the fuller development of the art but also the emergence of rival theories of composition. The paramount importance of Isocrates and of Aristotle in this regard was plainly recognized in antiquity and has not been seriously questioned since. Aristotle's handbook fortunately survives, but Isocrates has left us no formal treatise. Still, through a study of his own discourses it is possible to discern the general rules for his art that he had laid down and taught to his pupils for fifty years.

Isocrates was a great educator as well as a rhetorical theorist. His aim was not simply to turn young men into clever, but possibly unscrupulous, speakers, but to educate them to become good citizens. The intensive study of oratory was a means, not an end in itself, and underlying all formal education was the primary necessity of character building. He called his educational system "philosophy," and the end to be attained was civic excellence. To attain his purpose the educator must train his students in three directions: he must educate their intellect, their will, and their emotions. The three elements that entered into this training are the natural ability or disposition of the pupil, instruction, and practice. This threefold division had already been enunciated by the Sophists of the fifth century, notably by Protagoras; it became, so to speak, canonical from Isocrates' time on. The emphasis in Isocrates on the moral training of the student is of basic importance and recurs in all the best of the ancient educators. You will find it in Aristotle's *Rhetoric,* and it is implicit in Cicero's great treatise on the education of an orator. The elder Cato defined his ideal orator as "a good man skilled in speaking," and to Quintilian *probitas* is inseparable from true *eloquentia.* This fact deserves attention; for it is assuredly no accident that one of the oft-expressed aims of historians is the moral elevation of their readers.

Aristotle's manual on rhetoric is only in part concerned with the classification of speeches and with the formal rules to be followed in constructing a discourse. Its main importance and its originality are to be found even more in the emphasis placed on the relation between the speaker and his hearers. If the former is to practice persuasion with success, he must have a deep insight into human nature. Thus Aristotle analyzes different human emotions and different types of human character; only if he has a thorough knowledge of these will the orator or writer play successfully on the great instrument that is his audience.

History, then, must be composed according to artistic rules. A distinguished historian of our own day, in discussing the historians of the nineteenth century, differentiates between historians and men of letters, amongst whom he includes Macaulay and Carlyle.[9] Such a distinction would, I venture to say, have been meaningless to a Greek or a Roman. But if both alike agreed in regarding the writing of history as an art, there was less unanimity about the aims of historical composition. Whatever view may be taken of Polybius' animadversions on other historians, the amount of space that he devoted to this topic, involving also his own conception of how history should be written, is a clear, if indirect, proof that the whole question of historical writing was hotly debated in the Hellenistic age. And indeed why not? It is a subject of perennial interest and, since it concerns not merely the record but the interpretation of human affairs, and the further question of the best literary presentation, the problems and differences of opinion that are involved are in some respects still the same as they were in antiquity. Consider the following passage:

He wrote alike without the necessary amount of actual knowledge and without the necessary discipline of previous study. No doubt he laboured painfully and zealously at the materials for the period which he had immediately at hand; no doubt he brought to light much which had escaped the researches of earlier inquirers. But his natural defect combined with the lack of the needful previous education combined to make him incapable of using his own knowledge.... Men who understood the laws of criticism laughed at the ludicrous misapplications of evidence, and men who understood the laws of morality were indignant at the barefaced confusion of right and wrong.... Men who had spent their lives in the minute study of history smiled at the blunders in detail, the failure to understand the commonest words and names and things, which were, as commonly happens, conspicuous in one who undertook to set right all who had gone before him. Still the thing had a taking side. It was cleverly done; it pleased those to whom novelty is dearer than truth; it pleased those who took a pleasure in pretty talk about streams and blasts and daisies and dark November days and that mysterious clock which was always on the point of striking and yet never did strike.[10]

If the last sentence be disregarded, might one not seem to hear the stern accents of Polybius passing sentence on Timaeus? Actually the quoted passage was composed in 1864 and comes from one of Edward Freeman's more scathing attacks on Froude; yet the charges that he brings are in many ways similar to those leveled two thousand years before by one historian against others. But it was not only the right methods of historical inquiry that were debated; opinion varied also about the purpose of the finished product. Histories should give pleasure; they should serve as a guide to men of affairs and soldiers, from which they could learn what to do and what to avoid in any given set of circumstances; they should promote the moral improvement of the age and of the individual reader. Obviously these aims are not mutually exclusive. History might instruct and improve the mind and give pleasure too; it might be a handbook for statesmen and generals and also aid in the betterment of mankind. Polybius, as we have seen, criticized Phylarchus for putting the titillation of his readers above everything else; his own purpose was the very opposite of this. His *History* was in no sense intended to be popular; it was to be of practical use to leading men in civil and military life. Whatever we may think of this aim, we can only approve the broad requirements which a historical writer, according to Polybius, must fulfill. He must search for and sift sources and documents and must exercise his power of criticism on them; he must investigate the topography of the countries and events with which he deals; and he must have practical experience of warfare and of political life.

It has become customary in recent years to regard the type of historical writing associated with the names of Cleitarchus, Duris, or Phylarchus as a virtual invention of the Peripatetic school, but the arguments put forward in support of this view are far from convincing. Aristotle himself was careful to distinguish history from poetry, and says specifically: "The distinction between historian and poet is not in the one writing prose and the other verse—you might put the work of Herodotus into verse and it would still be a species of history; it consists really in this, that the one describes the thing that has been, and the other the thing that might be. Hence poetry is something more philosophical and of graver import, since its statements are of the nature of universals, whereas those of history are singulars."[11] Again, he remarks in a later passage of the *Poetics,* where he is concerned with epic poetry, that "the structures of epic poetry and histories are not the same. A history has to deal not with one action, but with one period and all that has happened in that to one or more persons, however disconnected the several events may have been. Just as two events may take place at the same time, e.g., the sea-fight off Salamis and the battle with the Carthaginians in Sicily, without converging to the same end, so also of two consecutive events one may sometimes come after the other with no one end as their common issue."[12]

In the *Rhetoric,* where he is dealing with different types of discourse, Aristotle divides the examples that the orator must use into those that are historical and those that are invented. Those taken from history are harder to find, but, "if it is easier to find parallels in tales, nevertheless for deliberative speaking the parallels from history are more effective, since in the long run things will turn out in the future as they have actually turned out in the past."[13] This does not mean that Aristotle would have subscribed to the half-baked notion of what history is which is expressed in the popular phrase that history repeats itself. What it does imply is that pragmatic view of history which has its most consistent exponent in Polybius. The man of affairs must study the past in order to have a guide for his own public conduct, to profit by the wisdom and to avoid the mistakes of statesmen in the past. For the rest, we see that Aristotle in no uncertain terms distinguishes or even contrasts the spheres of the poet, tragic and epic, and of the historian. Furthermore, he leaves the impression on the reader's mind that history is little more than a chronicle of events, and he does not allow room for the interpretation of the past by the historical inquirer through the correlation of simultaneous or successive events or by the study of cause and effect in human affairs. Still, it is conceivable that in some work now lost he had entered more deeply into the question, what is history.

Aristotle himself, then, carefully differentiated the functions of tragic and epic poetry from those of history. But, it has been argued, his successors applied his theory of dramatic poetry to historical composition. The argument appears to run something like this: Certain Hellenistic historians dramatized their material greatly or even to excess. But at least one of these historians was a pupil of Theophrastus; therefore this dramatic or "tragic" style of writing history was an invention of the Peripatetics.[14] The syllogism is faulty, for it assumes that Duris wrote history in the way that he did because he had been a student of Theophrastus, and of this there is no shadow of proof. Moreover, to bolster this theory it is necessary to minimize significant features in the earlier writers of history and to rely very heavily on late critics like Dionysius of Halicarnassus. That Polybius compared Phylarchus' manner to that of a tragic poet proves nothing, and he himself (ii.56) repeats good Aristotelian doctrine when he concludes that the purpose of history and of tragedy is not the same. It was no new discovery in the Hellenistic age that the recording of human affairs offers opportunity for displaying situations of an intensely dramatic or epic character. There are plenty of episodes dramatically told in the pages of Herodotus. It is assuredly no accident that the Melian dialogue, the bluntest expression of Athenian imperialism, is immediately followed in Thucydides' *History* by an account of the Sicilian expedition. We need only read the story of Theramenes' last hours to see how keenly aware Xenophon was that real life could be as dramatic as any stage play. Nor was the passing of favorable or adverse judgments (*laudatio* and *vituperatio*) by the historian on his characters a novelty of the period after Alexander. We have the germs of it in Thucydides' famous estimates of Themistocles and Pericles, or even in his brief criticism of Cleon. Xenophon ends his account of Theramenes, who drank the poison cup with a jest on his lips, with the observation: "Yet I must deem it an admirable trait in the man's character, if at such a moment, when death confronted him, neither his wits forsook him, nor could the childlike sportiveness vanish from his soul."[15] Excellent, too, as throwing light on the character of his hero, is the graphic narrative of Agesilaus surveying his prisoners at Peiraeum.[16] Theopompus was constantly passing moral judgments on peoples and persons. Again, the introduction of digressions in a historical work, which lent variety and helped to assure the continued interest of the reader, was no novelty. Polybius goes out of his way to praise Ephorus for such digressions and for his sententious utterances. He himself, like Thucydides before him, exercised severe restraint. When he introduces an excursus, it is always strictly relevant to the matter in hand.[17] Some Hellenistic historians wrote sensationally in order to attract the greatest number of readers; but the danger of sacrificing truth to popular appeal was one against which Thucydides had already warned (i.22). Polybius was wroth with Theopompus for dilating on the scandals at the court of Philip II and with Timaeus for enlarging on the vices of Demochares and of Agathocles. It is a nice point how far a historian or biographer is justified in passing lightly over the moral obliquities of prominent persons. Polybius would have applauded Carlyle, who, after dealing with certain scandalous reports on the life of Frederick the Great found in the "Demon News-writer," ends characteristically: "Among the tragical platitudes of Human nature, nothing so fills a considering brother mortal with sorrow and despair, as this tendency of the common crowd in regard to its Great Men, whensoever, or almost whensoever the Heavens do, at long intervals, vouchsafe us, as their all including blessing, anything of such." Yet, if a man's private vices react in any way on his public career, their suppression by the historian may lead to a distortion of the truth.[18]

I have tried to prove from specific examples that some of the characteristics found in Hellenistic histories were not new, but can be shown to have existed, at least in rudimentary form, long before. The whole question is surely one of emphasis. The fault of men like Duris and Phylarchus was that they did not always draw a careful line between fact and fiction; nor need one doubt

that they were influenced by their familiarity with epic and dramatic poetry. Duris, at least, wrote a book on tragedy and another
on the Homeric poems. Probably the feature of histories written in Greek and Roman antiquity which has met with most
criticism in modern times, especially from self-styled scientific
historians, is the introduction of fictitious speeches into a historical narrative. As rhetorical theory and training concerned
themselves primarily with oratory, it is such speeches that most
obviously betray the influence of rhetoric on historical writing.
The truth, however, is that this influence goes much deeper. It
has left its mark on all parts of the composition: the straight narrative of events, the occasional digressions on a variety of topics
often loosely connected with the main theme, which was the
political and military history of a given period or geographical
area, the personal comments and judgments of the historian—
all this in addition to the actual orations put by the author into
the mouth of leading, and occasionally of subsidiary, characters.
To condemn these speeches outright is to betray a singular
ignorance of the real purpose behind this literary device when
properly used. It could be and sometimes was abused. Fashions,
too, change. Antiquity had its overrhetorical historians; we have
our economic determinists. It cannot be said that either the one
or the other has at all times served the cause of truth. Just as
the dramatic element in a given historical episode might be
overstressed to the point of perverting the recorded facts, so the
speeches in some ancient historians were no more than rhetorical
displays, commonplaces strung together not unskillfully, padded
out with historical and mythical *exempla* and spiced with sententious maxims. The better writers kept a rein on both their imagination and the literary facility which they had learned in the
schools. Their speeches, as we shall see in authors like Livy and
Tacitus, served a very real purpose in enlightening their readers
about the character and policy of historical personages.[19]

It is easy to see that when the desire to compose a history according to the canons of artistic prose, as then understood, was joined to a historical imagination which fastened on the dramatic incidents of a particular period or on the clash of conflicting personalities which is of the very essence of drama, the result would be a presentation of the past heightened in color and divergent from, and fuller than, the bare factual and documentary record at the historian's disposal. But was the broad result necessarily false? If we reject as no better than fiction the famous chapters describing the flight to, and return from, Varennes, or the last hours of Marie Antoinette, or the vivid pages that bring before us the trial of the nonjuring bishops, if, in short, we believe that these familiar passages in Carlyle and Macaulay are unworthy of a sober historian, then we shall also throw into the discard Livy's portrayal of the suicide of the Capuan aristocrats, or Tacitus' lost narrative of Sejanus' fall or the death of Agrippina, or the closing scenes in the life of Julian as related by Ammianus. That there was a grave danger in the undisciplined use of the historical imagination the best of the ancient critics were well aware. Cicero contrasts the death of Themistocles as soberly told by Thucydides with the absurd narrative of a Cleitarchus or a Stratocles, who made the exiled Athenian statesman sacrifice a bull and then end his own life by quaffing the blood of the victim.[20] With the spread of education in the Hellenistic world, both on the lower and the higher levels came a steady increase in the reading public and in the demand for lectures and public recitations. There was also a greater variation in taste. If a good proportion of the historical literature composed in that age had survived, we should almost certainly find a far greater variety and gradation from very good to very bad than can be deduced from the ancient critics that are extant; we should see, to speak in modern terms, that the dividing line between a history and a historical novel was sometimes, but only sometimes, blurred.

Although the attribution of the "tragic" or "pathetic" type of history to the Lyceum is of questionable validity, it is nevertheless certain that much more attention was paid to antiquarian research, to biography, and to historical investigations over a wide field, in the Peripatetic school than in any of the other post-Aristotelian schools of philosophy. Neither the skepticism of the Middle or New Academy, which denied the possibility of knowledge, nor the self-centered life of contemplation, a kind of ancient Quietism, favored by and large by Epicurus and his followers, was calculated to further the spirit of inquiry for its own sake. But in the Lyceum the scientific approach and methods of its founder not only continued to be applied to the physical and biological sciences, but were extended also to the arts. Biography especially received much attention, and its subjects were not so much statesmen and soldiers as the philosophers and orators of bygone ages. It is obvious that these researches were bound very soon to influence historical writing, particularly when the foundations for a biographical approach to history had already been truly laid in the fourth century.

The influence of the Stoics was also deep, but it was more indirect. They did not wholly neglect the arts, and can be credited with some innovations in the field of rhetorical theory; but they did not, with the one notable exception of Posidonius, concern themselves greatly with history. Indirectly, however, their ethical teaching and their attitude to the established mythology and to official cults had a far-reaching effect on the thought of their contemporaries and successors. To the student of Roman historians this influence is of great moment, but, as will appear later, he must also be on his guard. By the Graeco-Roman period many ethical precepts and concepts, which may have originated with the earlier Stoics, though even this is not always certain, had undoubtedly become commonplaces and were taught not only in other philosophical schools but also by the professors of rhetoric.

It is, for example, quite futile, when we meet the antithesis between the expedient (*utile*) and the honorable (*honestum*) in a Roman historian, to assume a direct Stoic source for it.

In Polybius, the one Hellenistic historian of whose work substantial portions have survived, the effect of philosophical instruction in his youth is unmistakable.[21] It is also generally agreed that later in life, as an involuntary exile in Italy, he came under the influence of the leading Stoic of the day, Panaetius. It is dangerous, however, for the reasons already stated, to attribute Polybius' at times strongly moralistic tone exclusively to Stoic sources. The result of a fuller acquaintance with Stoic teaching is more apparent in certain sections of his book where he postulates for human affairs or institutions a theory of cycles of growth and decay parallel to that which was the foundation of the Stoic cosmology. In much of his *History* he seems to accept the vulgar belief in Fortune which affects the lives and affairs of men in unpredictable ways, although the form in which he adopted this view was apparently the quasi-philosophical one expounded by Demetrius of Phalerum.[22] It is one of several proofs that he did not live long enough to revise his book thoroughly, that elsewhere he repudiates Fortune and seeks for purely mundane causes.[23] Yet it is permissible to ask whether Tyche, as used by Polybius in at least one passage, is really very different from the Stoic Pronoia or Providence. Near the beginning of his book Polybius writes as follows:

There is this analogy between the plan of my History and the marvelous spirit of the age with which I have to deal. Just as Fortune made almost all the affairs of the world incline in one direction, and forced them to converge upon one and the same point, so it is my task as a historian to put before my readers a compendious view of the part played by Fortune in bringing about the general catastrophe. It was this peculiarity which originally challenged my attention, and determined me to undertake the work. And combined with this was the fact that no writer of my time has undertaken a general history.[24]

This passage bears a generic resemblance to another, which is found in Diodorus but is certainly derived from Posidonius:

Furthermore, it has been the aspiration of these writers [i.e., those who have written universal histories] to marshal all men, who although united one to another by their kinship, are yet separated by space and time, into one and the same orderly body. And such historians have therein shown themselves to be, as it were, ministers of Divine Providence. For just as Providence, having brought the orderly arrangement of the visible stars and the natures of men together into one common relationship, continually directs their courses through all eternity, apportioning to each that which falls to it by the direction of fate, so likewise the historians, in recording the common affairs of the inhabited world as though they were those of a single state, have made of their treatises a single reckoning of past events and a common clearing-house of knowledge concerning them.[25]

Posidonius, a man of unusual erudition who wrote on many topics, composed a historical work which apparently continued Polybius from 146 to 81 B.C. or perhaps a little later. In spite of all the notice that he has received at the hands of scholars during the past fifty or sixty years, he is still something of an enigma; and more recently a reaction has set in against the extravagant claims once made for him and the elaborate reconstructions of his thought which were the result. Professedly Posidonius was a Stoic, and he succeeded Panaetius as the acknowledged head of that school. But he was unlike other Stoics in his relative neglect of ethics and his preoccupation with scientific subjects like astronomy and physical geography. If we may take as typical a lengthy verbal citation from his *History* that happens to be embedded in the pages of a later author, he wrote in an unusually easy and flowing style enlivened by occasional irony and even a slightly mordant humor.[26] Furthermore, he was unorthodox in his attitude toward the significance in human life of various kinds of supernatural phenomena, such as visions, omens, and divination; for, though orthodox Stoics tried valiantly to find a place for such manifestations within their determinist scheme of the universe, Posidonius went much further.[27] His belief in a spirit world classes him with the mystics. It will be necessary to return to this topic in a later lecture in connection with certain passages in Livy.

One other question, important here because of its recurrence in the Roman historians, deserves brief mention. The broad statement has often been made that the idea of human progress was alien to the thought of pagan antiquity, that on the contrary the few thinkers who speculated about the evolution of human society were in effect, though not in name, pessimists. Present manners and institutions, according to this view, were judged by them adversely in comparison with those of a happier age. This is not the place to discuss what is certainly an oversimplification of a rather complex topic; but two points need to be stressed because of their bearing on the subject of these lectures. In the first place, one must distinguish what may be called philosophical theories about primitive society and an age of innocence long past from the disposition, as common now as in antiquity, to estimate the present unfavorably in comparison with the past. Philosophical theories on this theme were not the exclusive product of any one school; Plato, the Peripatetic Dicaearchus, Crates of Mallus, and Posidonius, all touched on the question. On the other hand, the tendency of middle and old age to be critical of youth is not only a trait of human nature, but in literature became a commonplace at a very early date. The elderly Nestor in the *Iliad,* who was far from complimentary about the younger warriors in the Greek camp opposite Troy, has his counterpart in Demosthenes comparing to their disadvantage the Athenians of his own day with the fighters at Marathon. When, therefore, we find a historian critical of his own times, and in contrast praising the good old days, we must not at once assume that he is writing in this strain because he holds some philosophical theory about degeneration or because his liver is temporarily out of order. He may simply be employing a well-established rhetorical antithesis.

Secondly, theories about primitive society show a good deal of variation. The best known, which is as old as Hesiod, postulated an original Golden Age from which all subsequent ages of man progressively declined. A variant of this hypothesis was imagined by Posidonius. His Golden Age was one in which government was in the hands of sages and Law only became needful when vices crept in and the government by the wise degenerated into despotism.[28] A rival theory to that of the Golden Age developed early. According to this, men were at one time little better than beasts. They owed their gradual transformation into civilized groups and organized societies to Law. This Law is at first regarded as a gift of the gods, be it Kronos or Zeus. But already by the second half of the fifth century the rationalism of Sophists like Protagoras explained the spread of Justice and Law not as due to a divine gift, but to human intelligence and effort.[29]

I have tried to indicate the general trend of historical writing in the Hellenistic world and to show that many of its characteristics were rooted in classical antiquity. At the same time it has been necessary to warn against certain common assumptions, especially against the bogey of rhetoric, which is so often raised by those who have not taken the trouble to distinguish between the ancient meaning of the term and its prevalent modern use in a derogatory sense, and who have failed to understand that to all the ancients, even to Thucydides, a certain literary form and excellence were an integral part of historical composition. In history the influence on Rome of Greece was as unmistakable as it was in poetry and oratory. And, though the historical works of Sallust and his successors retained certain characteristically national traits, the Hellenic leaven had been at work in the Roman meal long before.

## CHAPTER II

# ROMAN HISTORIANS TO THE
# DEATH OF CAESAR

HISTORICAL writing in prose began in Rome nearly fifty years
after the first poet and translator, Livius Andronicus, had begun
to bring out his works. From the end of the second war with
Carthage to the age of Cicero and Caesar it had many practi-
tioners; but, although some record has survived of two dozen
or more, a good proportion of these are little more than names.
Even of the others it is difficult to judge fairly, unless we are
prepared to indulge in preconceived theories; for the available
material is scanty. Direct quotations in later writers are few.
Often, when the authority of an annalist is invoked, it is uncertain whether more than a bare statement or the gist of an argument is in question. To speak plainly, the whole problem has
been thoroughly bedeviled by the "Quellenforscher"; we shall
meet it again in aggravated form when we consider historians
like Livy and Tacitus. For the present it is enough to observe that
any attempt to form a clear estimate of an author like Fabius
Pictor from the study of a highly rhetorical writer like Dionysius
of Halicarnassus, who lived a century and a half later, is little
short of fantastic. It is possible by this approach to gain some
notion of the topics treated by Fabius in different sections of his
book and to note controversial points on which he differed from
other annalists, but beyond this it is unsafe to go.

It is possible to group these historical writers in various ways,
especially if antiquarians are to be included under the general
heading of Republican historiography. Thus one may distinguish the earlier annalists, the later, more popular authors from
the age of the Gracchi on, and the "professional researchers" of
the first century before Christ.[1] It is an easy classification, but in

[1] For notes to chapter ii, see pages 166–169.

some ways unsatisfactory, because it does not take into sufficient account either the varying subject matter of the books or their style and method of composition. The great majority of these writers set out to give a general account of Roman history from the beginnings down to their own time. Claudius Quadrigarius, however, deviated from the established practice; he ignored the earliest centuries and began with the sack of Rome by the Gauls in 387 B.C. It was natural that all these men treated the later portions of their annals more fully than the earlier, a procedure which had its parallel in a Greek author like Ephorus. The evidence that they could gather for the regal and early Republican periods was far less in quantity and far poorer in quality than what was available for the later fourth and third centuries. Besides, we may suspect that in Rome, as in Hellenistic or even in classical Greece, interest was keener in contemporary or near-contemporary history. It was not until the last decades of the second century that detailed accounts of briefer historical periods came into fashion. Coelius Antipater concentrated his attention on the Second Punic War, while Sempronius Asellio, who had served as a young officer under Scipio Aemilianus at the siege of Numantia, subsequently wrote a history of his own times. A generation later, Sisenna composed a history of the Italian and civil wars between 91 and 82, a work which Sallust with certain reservations admired and continued in his own *Histories*.[2] But the troubled times through which Rome passed in the last quarter of the second and the first quarter of the first century were not only portrayed in the concluding sections of general annals or in special monographs; they also received partisan treatment in the published reminiscences of prominent personages. We know of at least four such works, the memoirs of Aemilius Scaurus, Rutilius Rufus, Catulus, and Sulla.

The earlier annalists aimed at conciseness of treatment; their successors, beginning with Gellius and Claudius Quadrigarius, provided their readers with fuller, though not necessarily more accurate, narratives. Several deeply rooted misconceptions about these authors call for brief discussion. In the first place, the use of the word "annals," which was applied also to national epics like that of Ennius, does not mean that these historical accounts were no more than bare lists of magistrates, elections, and noteworthy events, without any pretense to literary form. The name "annals" implies merely that the work followed more or less strictly chronological order.[2] Again, the earlier annalists, Fabius Pictor, Acilius, Cincius, Scipio, son of the Elder Africanus, and Postumius Albinus, composed their works in Greek and not in Latin. The reason for this choice of a foreign language, it used to be said, was that Latin prose had not yet developed and in fact began only with Cato the Censor. It is surely surprising that so preposterous an assertion should so long have held the field. Any reader of Cicero's *Brutus* is aware that it contains a long list of early Roman worthies who in their day had been famous as public speakers. Cicero is careful to add: "I do not pretend to have historical evidence that the persons here mentioned were then reckoned orators or that any sort of reward or encouragement was given to eloquence. I only infer what seems very probable."[3] One of these speeches from an earlier age, that delivered by Appius Claudius in 280 B.C., in which he had urged the Roman senate to reject the peace proposals of Pyrrhus, survived and was known to Cicero. Moreover, all the earlier annalists about whom we possess any information had held public office. They were members of Rome's governing class, they were accustomed to debate, and used to reading and drafting public documents. The number of official records that had accumulated by the time of Fabius Pictor was probably substantial. Tenney Frank was right in insisting on their importance to the earlier annalists, though he perhaps inclined to exaggerate the total amount of such material that was available. He also deserves our gratitude for pointing out repeatedly that the total destruction of early treaties and records in the Gaulish sack of Rome has been disproved by archaeological evidence. It is therefore absurd to assume that Fabius used Greek as his medium of expression because he could not express himself properly in Latin. His real reason for choosing Greek was in all likelihood the desire to reach a particular audience. His book was intended primarily to provide Greek readers with some knowledge of Roman history at a time when Rome was being brought more directly into political relations with the Greeks across the sea. Likewise, a long residence in Greek-speaking Sicily may have influenced Acilius' choice. Why Cincius and Scipio did the same must remain unexplained; it may have been mere imitation of their predecessors, or they also may have had Greek readers in mind. It may even have been mere affectation, as in Albinus, who for this reason incurred the sarcasm of Cato.[5]

The *Origines* of that remarkable man stand somewhat apart from other historical works, and their loss is greatly to be deplored. Cato composed them in his later years, and ancient writers testify to the care which he took to attain accuracy.[6] When he was unable to obtain information that seemed to him sufficiently reliable, he did not hesitate to admit his ignorance.[7] When completed, the *Origines* comprised seven Books; but the title, strictly speaking, suited only the first three, which dealt with the early history, geography, and ethnology of Rome and other Italian communities. Books IV to VII related the military, and to a less extent the political, history of Rome from the First Punic War down to the Lusitanian War of 149 B.C. Although he published his speeches separately, he also included a few in the *Origines*. In the later Books he did not hesitate to speak freely of his own achievements or to attack political opponents with some asperity. Of the 143 fragments collected by Peter, approximately half come from Books I to III. Most of the fragments are very brief, and exact verbal citations are few; but two longer passages from the later Books survive in Aulus Gellius, thanks to the archaizing tastes of the Antonine age.[8]

Sparse as is the material available for the study of this historical literature, it is enough to justify certain general conclusions. The earlier annalists and Cato, though they did not waste words, in a phrase or two might incidentally convey interesting information and even set the reader to wondering about the hobbies of the writer. From a brief fragment of Fabius Pictor it appears that female swallows were trained and used in a way resembling the modern employment of carrier pigeons.[9] Cato, the expert farmer, had an appreciative eye for the sows raised in Cisalpine Gaul, which were too fat to walk and had to be taken to market in a cart. We can picture him, too, on the rare occasions when he allowed himself a little leisure, relaxing with rod and line in Spain or Dalmatia, even though economic historians may solemnly assure us that he was only interested in the commercial exploitation of the rivers Ebro and Naro.[10] Both the earlier and the later annalists recorded supernatural phenomena like dreams and prodigies; they occurred in Fabius Pictor as well as in Gellius, Coelius, who was very partial to such things, and Sisenna.[11] Among the later compilers, whose treatment of their subject was more elaborate, Claudius Quadrigarius was distinguished by a simple, easy style, and his reference to "whinnying mares raising clouds of dust with their hooves" shows that he had an observant eye and some gift for describing natural scenes.[12] The great, indeed the excessive, length of the later annals was achieved by including much material from unofficial sources. Family records were consulted and this sometimes led to a perversion of the truth. If we knew more, we should probably find that oral tradition was drawn on extensively. It is easy in these days to forget how great a part this played in antiquity. Learning by heart and passing on what one had thus acquired to the next generation was a regular method of preserving a knowledge of the remoter past. Such traditions would lack the precision of an official record written down at the time when the events recorded occurred; but it is quite erroneous to assume that these traditions were necessarily false in the main facts that they handed down. It is also easy to exaggerate the degree to which the younger annalists allowed their loyalty to a particular family or *gens* to color their entire presentation of past events. The presence or suspicion of such a bias should make us wary; but it should not lead us to reject the writer's testimony on all points, and a writer like Licinius Macer deserves more consideration than he has usually received.[13]

We can also gain some insight from the fragments into the general method and approach of these authors. Sempronius Asellio apparently prided himself on his historical outlook and regarded the annals compiled before his time as no better than tales for children.[14] To illustrate the strict discipline enforced by Roman generals on active service, which had been one of the reasons for Rome's military successes, he introduced a story about a Roman commander and the official of an allied state at the siege of Leucas.[15] Both Claudius and Valerius Antias related the plot to murder Pyrrhus of Epirus, and Claudius even inserted into his narrative a letter from the senate to the king.[16] Valerius, whose exaggerations, especially of casualties and booty taken in time of war, Livy was later to pillory, seems to have gone farther than most in mingling fact with fiction, with the deliberate aim of pleasing the groundlings, rather in the manner of certain unsavory biographers in our own day. Thus he was the only ancient historian to throw doubt on the continence of Scipio Africanus, his sole source of information for the libel being apparently some scurrilous verses of the poet Naevius.[17] He also was responsible for the false account of a shameful episode in the life of L. Quinctius Flamininus. A charge of immoral conduct was originally directed against him by Cato in a speech delivered before the senate; but it was the more lurid version of Antias which prevailed and which reappears again and again in later centuries.[18]

The interrelation of these writers, taken as a whole, need not long detain us. It is certain, and this is only what was to be expected, that later annalists used their Roman predecessors, as, for example, Licinius Macer was indebted to Gellius. A more important and also a more difficult question is whether they consulted Greek historians. That Coelius Antipater borrowed from Silenus, the Sicilian or Campanian writer who had composed a history of the Hannibalic War from the Carthaginian point of view, is a fact that rests not merely on indirect evidence but on the express statement of Cicero. It is highly probable that both Fabius Pictor and Cato made some use of Timaeus in the earlier sections of their works. Cato's famous remark that eminent men should be judged as much by the way in which they spent their leisure as by their conduct of affairs may have been original. But the sentiment occurs already in Xenophon; it may also have become a commonplace of the schools after his time.[19] Piso, the annalist who had been consul in 133 B.C., gave his readers a derivation of the name "Italia" which goes back to Timaeus and reappears in Varro; but Piso may have obtained his information from a Roman predecessor.[20] Timaeus' date, on the other hand, for the foundation of Rome was not accepted by Roman writers, who also disagreed amongst themselves. Fabius had placed the event in the year 748, Cincius in 729, but Timaeus had moved it back to 814, while the poet Ennius seems to have favored a date earlier by almost a century than that of Timaeus.[21]

If occasional glimpses into Roman historical literature before Caesar and Sallust are more tantalizing than a palimpsest, they can at least be supplemented by the views on history and on historical writing expressed by the greatest literary figure in the late

Republic. Cicero in his *De oratore* maintains emphatically that a knowledge of history is essential for an orator, or, as we should say, for a public man. The rules for historical writing are set before the reader: strict adherence to truth, impartiality, a proper presentation of facts, an understanding of the main causes and the contributing factors that have produced important events and situations in the past, and the life and manners of the principal actors on the stage of history.[22] But history is an art; therefore Cicero also demands that certain canons of style and composition be observed. This leads him to lament the absence of historical works in Latin which fulfilled all requirements. He alludes more than once both to the earlier and to the later annalists and to writers of monographs like Coelius. Thus Antonius in the dialogue remarks: "It is far from surprising if history has not yet made a figure in our language; for none of our countrymen study eloquence, unless that it may be displayed in litigation and in the forum; whereas among the Greeks the most eloquent men, wholly unconnected with public pleading, applied themselves to other honorable studies as to writing history."[23] It is noticeable that Cicero in this passage mentions no Greek historian later than Timaeus; but elsewhere, while speaking of Sisenna, he brings in Cleitarchus, an allusion that is rather obscure. This passage also contains a sentence that has consistently been mistranslated or misinterpreted by modern critics. Atticus, who is one of the speakers in the *De legibus* as Antonius is in *De oratore,* laments the absence of history from the national literature. He urges Cicero to undertake a historical work *quippe cum sit, ut tibi quidem videri solet, unum hoc oratorium maxime—*"because history, as you certainly are accustomed to maintain, demands above all a fully developed prose style." This, I submit, is the correct rendering of a sentence which too often has been misused to prove that Cicero regarded the writing of history as no more than a rhetorical exercise.[24] What Cicero does

mean, therefore, and in this he is in line with the Greeks of the
classical and Hellenistic periods, is that the true historian must
be an artist; "oratory" in the wider meaning in which he employs
the word is synonymous with "artistic prose." It is significant that,
when he criticizes earlier Roman historians, he is almost always
concerned with literary form. "History then was nothing but
a compilation of annals." Its authors "neither understand how
composition is to be adorned (for ornaments of style have been
but recently introduced among us) and, provided what they
related can be understood, think brevity of expression the only
merit. Antipater, an excellent man, the friend of Crassus, raised
himself a little and gave history a higher tone; the others did
not give a literary form to their facts, but were content with mere
narration." The annalists whom Cicero names in this connection are Cato, Fabius Pictor, and Piso, whose annals he once
dubbed "baldly composed" (*exiliter scriptos*). He has less to
say about the younger annalists, but he judged Licinius Macer
severely, probably for personal or political reasons. As for Cato
the Censor, he is not wholly consistent, for in the *Brutus* (63–66)
he vouchsafes him the highest praise, *considering the time at
which he lived*. He is, of course, thinking primarily of Cato as
an orator, but remarks of the *Origines* "that they were adorned
with every flower and with all the lustre of eloquence." The
discrepancy between Cicero's views in *De oratore* and in the
*Brutus* is more apparent than real. In *De oratore* his main concern is the fully developed art of prose composition. Judged by
this standard the writers of the second century, even Cato, were
still crude as artists, although Cato might be naturally eloquent,
incisive, witty, or sarcastic, as occasion demanded. But in the
*Brutus* Cicero's theme is the historical development of oratory,
Greek and Roman, and he rightly emphasizes the supremely
important place of Cato in this development. Cicero's comparison of the Censor with Lysias, whose style was admirable for

its purpose, but simple and unadorned in comparison with the stately periods of Isocrates or the impassioned stream of Demosthenes' eloquence, is a clear indication of his meaning in this passage. He was well aware that history could easily be falsified. The annalists had certain official records to consult, if they chose—treaties with other states, laws and resolutions passed by the senate, and the notations made year by year by the pontifical college. But, besides these, there were private records, more especially funeral orations pronounced from time to time over members of the leading Roman families and handed down from generation to generation. About these Cicero remarks: "The true version of our history has been corrupted by these panegyrics. They contain many occurrences that never took place, false triumphs, successive consulships (attributed to one man), even fictitious relationships and transfers from patrician to plebeian families, when persons of humbler origin were introduced into another clan of the same name." A generation later, Livy was to utter a similar warning in a passage which, though it bears no verbal resemblance, may well be a conscious reminiscence of Cicero.[25]

So far we have considered only those observations of Cicero's which are concerned with historical composition in the strict sense. But there is one pronouncement by him which cannot be ignored, but which seems to deal with a special topic. In 60 B.C. he had approached Posidonius and sent him a memoir on his consulship, hoping that the Greek historian would give a full account of that *annus mirabilis;* but Posidonius had politely declined. Then, in the spring of 56 B.C., when Cicero's relations with the so-called Triumvirs were very strained and he was compelled, not without much bitterness of feeling, to abandon the policy of active and public opposition which he had announced soon after his return from exile, he not unnaturally thought back again to the services that he had rendered to his country in 63 B.C. In this mood he wrote to L. Lucceius, Caesar's unsuccessful running-mate for the consulship of 59, who had turned historian and was engaged on a history of Rome beginning with the war between Rome and her Italian allies from 91 to 88.[20] After complimenting Lucceius on that part of his work that had already appeared, he asks him whether, instead of including the events of Cicero's consulship in due course in his *History,* he would not consider composing a separate monograph to which the strict rule of impartiality necessary in a historical work would not apply. But let us hear Cicero's own words:

From the beginning of the conspiracy to my return from exile it seems to me that a fair-sized volume could be compiled, in which you will be able to make use of your exceptional knowledge of civil changes, whether in disentangling the causes of the revolution or suggesting remedies for its calamities, while you reprehend what you consider blameworthy, and justify what you approve, setting forth your reasons in either case; and if you think you should treat the subject with exceptional freedom of speech, as has been your habit, you will stigmatize the disloyalty, intrigues, and treachery of which many have been guilty towards me. Moreover, what has happened to me will supply you with an infinite variety of material, abounding in a sort of pleasurable interest which could powerfully grip the attention of the reader—if you are the writer. For there is nothing more apt to delight the reader than the manifold changes of circumstance, and vicissitudes of fortune, which, however undesirable I found them to be in my own experience, will certainly afford entertainment in the reading; for the placid recollection of a past sorrow is not without its charm.

The rest of the world, however, who have passed through no sorrow of their own, but are the untroubled spectators of the disasters of others, find a pleasure even in their pity. Take, for instance, the way the great Epaminondas died at Mantinea; who of us but recalls it with delight, mingled with a certain compassion? Then only does he bid them pluck out the javelin, when in answer to his question he is told that his shield is safe; and so, despite the agony of the wound, with a mind at ease he died a glorious death. Who does not feel his sympathy excited and sustained in reading of the exile and return of Themistocles? The fact is that the regular chronological record of events in itself interests us as little as if it were a catalogue of historical occurrences; but the uncertain and varied fortunes of a statesman who frequently rises to prominence give scope for surprise, suspense, delight, annoyance, hope, fear; should those fortunes, however, end in some striking consummation, the result is complete satisfaction of mind which is the most perfect pleasure a reader can enjoy.

The desire to place Cicero as a man and an author in an unfavorable light has warped the judgment of not a few of his modern critics. But Cicero's meaning is clear and unexceptionable. Earlier in this same letter he had mentioned by way of general comparison three Greek works, Callisthenes' *Phocian War,* Timaeus' *War of Pyrrhus,* and Polybius' *Numantine War.* His point is that a brief period is suitable for monographic treatment. Later on he alludes to Xenophon's *Life of Agesilaus* and to the favorable portraits of Timoleon and Themistocles drawn respectively by Timaeus and by Herodotus. He is also perfectly frank with Lucceius, inviting him to show partiality or, to quote his own words once more, "to eulogize my actions with even more warmth than perhaps you feel and in that respect to disregard the canons of history (*leges historiae*)." Cicero, as we have already seen, knows perfectly well what "the laws of history" are. Here he is proposing to Lucceius that he write a monograph around a central figure. He will, if he composes the kind of book that Cicero has in mind, be free to heighten the dramatic elements in the story and appeal to certain deep-rooted psychological reactions in his readers; and he will set aside the strict objectivity necessary in his *Annals* and weight the scales in favor of his central character. All this is clear enough to anyone who reads the letter without preconceptions; but if he have any lingering doubts, then surely Cicero's antithesis between *perpetuam rerum gestarum historiam,* that is, Lucceius' general history of the times, and *hanc quasi fabulam rerum eventorumque nostrorum,* namely the proposed monograph, must surely dispel them. The book is to be, as it were, a drama. It will thus, it may be added, have characteristics similar to those of a certain type of Hellenistic history. Cicero does not say this, nor is there any reason to suppose that he would have approved this kind of dramatization in a strictly historical work. The monograph, though not a biography, will emphasize the biographical aspect of its theme; it will also have some of the features belonging to the encomium, a recognized literary form since the days of Isocrates. Cicero's observations, then, in this letter display great psychological insight, but they must not be taken as part of his judgment about the laws of history. It is surely an example of academic blindness to the world in which we live that this letter has so frequently been misjudged. Biographies and studies of prominent men still living are published almost every year. Such books may be no more than uncritical eulogies, but they may also have considerable value, provided the reader understands that the author's estimate of his hero and of the events in which he played a part cannot, in the nature of the case, be definitive or even impartial.

Time and chance have dealt unkindly with the autobiographical literature of the first century before Christ. Greece produced the prototype of this class of composition. The *Memoirs* of Aratus of Sicyon, though not the first, were the outstanding example of this genre.[27] They were consulted by Polybius and praised by him for their clearness and veracity. Plutarch drew on them extensively and regarded them as trustworthy, although in one place he criticized Aratus' account; and it is to Plutarch that we owe most of what we know of the *Memoirs.* It is from Plutarch also that we obtain most of our knowledge about Sulla's *Reminiscences.* They were lengthy, for at the time of his death he had just completed the twenty-second Book. If one of these Books was approximately as long as one Book of Caesar's *Commentaries,* then the *Reminiscences* must have been twice as long as the *Gallic* and *Civil Wars* together. Sulla's work was used by Plutarch both for the life of the dictator and for his biography of Marius. It is clear that the book was far from being objective, and Plutarch states that Sulla used the opportunity to justify after the event the more questionable episodes in his career. Sulla also affected to attribute his many successes to Fortune and, in support of this claim, recorded many portents and supernatural phenomena. As Plutarch dryly observes: "He gave the honor of all to Fortune, whether it were out of boastfulness or a real feeling of divine agency." Sulla advised Lucullus, to whom the *Reminiscences* were dedicated, to "esteem nothing more trustworthy than what the divine powers advise him by night." Indeed, the dictator applied this principle to his chief opponent.[28] As the first century progressed, a substantial body of autobiographical literature accumulated. If only Caesar's two famous books have survived, we may suspect that it was not chance alone but the deliberate choice of posterity which was responsible.

Although the *Commentaries* may be said to belong generically to the same class of literature as the *Reminiscences* of men like Rutilius Rufus, Catulus, and Sulla, there were also notable points of difference. The works of Sulla and the others, so far as they were *pièces justificatives,* had as their deliberate aim the defense of the writer's past conduct. Caesar's seven Books *De bello Gallico,* whatever view is taken of their method of composition, were available to the reading public at the latest in 50 B.C., and consequently before hostilities between Caesar and Pompey had begun or Caesar had attained to supreme power. Not a few modern critics have argued that both *Commentaries,* so far from being objective presentations of Caesar's campaigns, were disguised political pamphlets. According to this interpretation, the *De bello Gallico* was a defense against Cato and other embittered opponents in the senate, who charged Caesar with being guilty of wanton aggressions in Gaul; similarly, the *De bello civili* was a clever attempt to shift the primary responsibility for the civil war from his own shoulders to those of Pompey. An autobiographical book, if it were rigidly objective, would be neither interesting nor convincing. If neither the personality of the writer nor his aims and aspirations but only his actions are revealed, the result will be all but valueless. But it is one thing to say that the two *Commentaries* were composed from Caesar's point of view, quite another to maintain that they deliberately falsified history. One of the profoundest students of Caesar in our time, the late Rice Holmes, observed very pertinently that it has been precisely those moderns who from long military experience were in the best position to judge the *Commentaries on the Gallic War* who have been loudest in their praise of them.[29] Hostile critics are too often reduced to giving undue weight to the statements of Plutarch or Dio, as though their testimony were of equal weight with Caesar's. This type of pundit should be set the task of composing an intelligible account of the conquest of Gaul, using only Plutarch. The result would be grotesque. The older view, that the *De bello Gallico* was composed and published as a single whole, has frequently been challenged in recent years. An increasing number of scholars now incline to the view that the seven Books were issued one by one, as each campaigning season ended. The adoption of this hypothesis, which I cannot regard as finally proved, at least weakens still further the arguments of those who interpret the *Commentaries* as a glorified political manifesto.[30]

Most of the criticisms leveled against Caesar's narrative on the score of accuracy, personal glorification, or partiality break down on closer examination. Even in the *Commentaries on the Civil War* the unprejudiced reader will find it hard to discover deliberate falsification of evidence; but he will encounter passages where Caesar's memory of past events was at fault. Caesar may have exaggerated the losses of Pompey at the battle of Pharsalus and minimized his own; but is there any proof that Asinius Pollio was an accurate observer?[31] Again, it shows a lack of insight amounting to perversity to maintain that Caesar lied when he said that he addressed his troops at Ravenna before leading them on to the invasion of Italy, and that he only divulged his plans after he had crossed the Rubicon. When we consider how much depended on the loyalty of his men, we may be sure that he took them into his confidence before he took the irrevocable step. That he addressed them again before the actual fighting is likely enough, but he saw no reason for mentioning this. Besides, it is difficult to see what he could have hoped to gain by deliberately misrepresenting facts familiar to so many of his contemporaries. It was no way to strengthen his position before he attained to power nor to increase his authority or prestige after he had become master of the Roman world.

If there is one quality which predominates in all Caesar's writing it is restraint—the absence of hyperbole in ideas or language. What, for example, could be simpler or less emotional than this passage from the *Civil War?*[32]

Achillas, relying on these troops and despising the small number of Caesar's men, was in process of occupying Alexandria, save for that part of the city held by Caesar and his soldiers. At the first onset he had tried to burst into Caesar's house, but Caesar had distributed cohorts about the streets and held his assault in check. At the same time a fight took place near the harbor and that action resulted in by far the heaviest fighting. For there were at the same time encounters between forces scattered through many streets, and the enemy in great numbers were striving to seize the war galleys, of which fifty had been sent to help Pompey and after the engagement in Thessaly had returned home. All of them were quadriremes and quinqueremes serviceable and equipped in every way for navigation. In addition to these there were twenty-two, all of them fenced,[33] which had usually been stationed for garrison duty in Alexandria. If the enemy had seized these, they would, by depriving Caesar of his fleet, have become masters of the harbor and the entire shore line and would have cut him off from supplies and reinforcements. For this reason the action was fought with the intensity that was bound to occur when one side saw that a quick victory, the other their own safety, hung on the issue. But Caesar attained his object. He burnt all those galleys and the rest that were in the docks because he could not with his small army protect so extensive an area; and he at once got his men on board and disembarked them on Pharos.

The facts are allowed to speak for themselves, and the effect is cumulative. Caesar is greatly outnumbered but makes the most of his resources. The street fighting is violent, for so much hangs on victory or defeat. Finally, in an all but desperate situation, Caesar takes the heroic step of destroying the fleet and so staking everything on his ability to withstand a siege until adequate help can arrive.

Military reversals or near-disasters are not glossed over, and the attentive reader is led by sheer sequence of events to the highest degree of tension, as he is made aware, step by step, of the heavy odds against which the legionaries were contending in their campaign against the Nervii or the all but superhuman efforts by which the general and his men partly retrieved their failure at Gergovia. Nor does Caesar forget to show how a chance occurrence, lucky or unlucky, may in time of war have results out of all proportion to the event itself. Caesar's splendid audacity in blockading Pompey at Petra came very near indeed to success, but failed eventually as much owing to his difficulty in feeding his men for a protracted period as because of Pompey's superior numbers. In the last stage of the fighting an error committed by one body of his troops nearly brought complete disaster on his entire army. Caesar introduces this episode with a brief reflection: "Chance, which exerts the greatest influence in all circumstances, but especially in war, by slightly shifting the balance produces far-reaching changes in the affairs of men."[34] A little later, when

Pompey fails to follow up his success immediately, Caesar reflects on the reasons for this and again alludes to Fortune: "In this way small events have often turned the scale of Fortune to success or failure. The defense lines extending from the camp to the river interrupted Caesar's victory which, after Pompey's camp had been stormed, was all but won, and the same obstacle by slowing down the swiftness of the pursuers brought safety to our troops."[85] With a few incisive words Caesar praises his officers for work well done, and few eminent commanders have been so well served by their staff. Occasional failures due to unforeseen contingencies or, what was rarer, inexperience and bad judgment, he comments on with forbearance or even with generosity. Titurius Sabinus' obstinate folly, which led to serious disaster as well as to his own death, is passed over without criticism. Quintus Cicero is praised for his courage and determination, and there is scarcely a hint of disapproval for his mistakes. Labienus' unquestioned eminence as a general stands out unmistakably again and again, as we read the bare recital of his achievements; and once Caesar goes further and shows his appreciation in a few restrained words. Labienus was the one important officer who changed sides in the civil war; his action must have hit Caesar hard on both personal and military grounds. Yet there is no bitter criticism in his later book. Labienus' military competence is as clearly portrayed in the *Civil War* as in the *Gallic War*. His ruthlessness is mentioned twice (iii.19 and 71) and, like that of other Pompeian officers, it is in marked contrast to Caesar's own leniency toward his Roman opponents. The implied comparison was doubtless intentional on Caesar's part. Labienus' loyalty to Pompey is stressed, with perhaps a hint that he had gained a certain ascendancy over his chief (iii.71 and 87). There is a touch of acid in Caesar's comment on his old colleague in 59 B.C. and political opponent, M. Bibulus, who was admiral-in-chief of the Adriatic in 48 B.C. on the side of Pompey: "For Bibulus, learning

at Corfu that Caesar was approaching, and hoping to be able
to fall in with some of the loaded transports, intercepted them
empty. Capturing about thirty of them, he vented on them his
rage caused by vexation at his own carelessness, and burnt them
all. In the same fire he killed the crews and commanders of the
vessels, hoping that the rest would be intimidated by the rigor
of the punishment."[36] Yet in the next sentence we are told that
Bibulus remained constantly on board ship and shirked no labor
or task; and a few chapters later Caesar lays stress on Bibulus'
devotion to duty and on the hardships that he endured, which
caused his death on active service.[37] And is there not generosity
in his final comment, which has almost the quality of an epitaph,
on Curio who had so sadly bungled the African campaign of
48 B.C.? "Cn. Domitius, prefect of cavalry, surrounding Curio
with a few troopers, urged him to seek safety in flight and hasten
to the camp; and he promised that he would not leave him. But
Curio declared that he would never come back to appear in
Caesar's presence after he had lost the army which he had received from him as a trust; and so he died fighting."[38]

As a writer Caesar had fashioned for himself a perfect medium
of expression. Cicero admired him profoundly as an orator, and
later Roman critics agreed with this estimate. But he also praised
highly the earlier of Caesar's two *Commentaries.* In truth, if a
mature reader find Caesar's books dull in content and monoto-
nous in expression, the fault does not lie with Caesar. Simplicity
and clarity in writing can be most deceptive, and there are few
authors to whom the hackneyed saying, *ars est celare artem,* can
more fittingly be applied. In a bare hundred words he succeeds
in explaining a plan of action and the purposes, military and
political, that lie behind it:

On receiving this information, Caesar laid his plans to suit the nature
of the ground. Pompey's camp was surrounded by many high rugged
hills. Caesar began by occupying these with detachments and building

. :doubts there. Then, taking advantage of the natural features of the locality, he drew a line of defense works from fort to fort and proceeded to invest Pompey. He had the following purposes in mind: first, since his own commissariat was scanty and Pompey had a great superiority in cavalry, he would be able to bring in grain and supplies for his army with less risk, and at the same time he would cut off Pompey from foraging and render his cavalry useless for actual fighting; and, thirdly, he would undermine the personal influence on which Pompey clearly relied above all among foreign nations, when the report had been bruited abroad far and wide that he was being blockaded by Caesar and did not venture to fight a pitched battle.[30]

Caesar was a complete master of rhetorical theory and its application. Much has been written on his extensive use of indirect discourse, but it is unwise to make dogmatic statements about it. Caesar's own addresses are invariably given in this form, but the later books of the *Gallic War* and the *Civil War* also contain speeches in *oratio recta*. Most of these in the earlier work are brief, for even Critognatus' oration (vii.77) runs to barely 350 words. The *Civil War,* although its narrative is as restrained and concise, seems nevertheless to exhibit somewhat greater elaboration in the reflective portions. The author's own speeches are again in *oratio obliqua,* but for other characters he has composed speeches in direct discourse. In so doing he adopted the recognized literary device of ancient historians, as though he would prove to his contemporaries that he could write history according to the established literary canons. Curio's speeches are completely appropriate, once the Greek and Roman convention regarding the introduction of speeches into historical works is understood. Caesar was not himself present in Africa, although he doubtless received from survivors a full account of the disastrous campaign against Juba. We need not suppose that anyone told him what Curio had said at a critical juncture; for what Caesar does is to put before his readers in this graphic manner the problems that confronted his subordinate in Africa and the solution for them that he proposed to adopt. Highly effective, if rhetorical, is the series of questions in *oratio obliqua* employed by Caesar in his description of a crucial moment in the masterly campaign at Ilerda. Stylistically this passage, which must be quoted in the original, appears to be unique in his *Commentaries:*

Caesar in eam spem venerat, se sine pugna et sine vulnere suorum rem conficere posse, quod re frumentaria adversarios interclusisset. Cur etiam secundo proelio aliquos ex suis amitteret? Cur vulnerari pateretur optime de se meritos milites? Cur denique fortunam periclitaretur? praesertim cum non minus esset imperatoris consilio superare quam gladio. Movebatur etiam misericordia civium quos interficiendos videbat; quibus salvis atque incolumibus rem obtinere malebat.[40]

No English translation can adequately reproduce the effect of the three short sharp questions, possible only in a highly inflected language like Latin. Equally striking is the way in which the emphatic word or phrase comes at the end of the sentence—*amitteret, optime de se meritos milites, periclitaretur, gladio,*—with the additional result that monotony of rhythm is avoided. Here then, compressed into sixty-four words, we have Caesar's three reasons for the course of action that he adopts, with a supplementary comment on each. He will avoid further casualties among his men, veterans who have served him with the utmost loyalty. He will avoid the unknown hazard of a second battle; for it is the function of the highest generalship to attain its object by policy or strategy as much as by actual combat. He will avoid further loss of life among citizens; for it is a civil war that he is fighting and the enemy too are Romans. Caesar's reasons are given, it would seem, in the order of their importance in his mind.

It has not been my purpose to attempt an evaluation of Caesar as a stylist, a task that other scholars are far more competent to perform. But some reference to Caesar the writer as distinct from Caesar the historical authority was inevitable. The best historians of modern times have in some respects progressed far beyond what was possible for the ancients. It would be both strange and sad if it were not so. But it is still as true now as in the days of Greece and Rome that the accumulation, sifting, and correlation of facts and their interpretation is not enough. To be numbered among the elect the historian must also achieve their clear and logical presentation; he must in the last analysis be not only a scholar but a creative artist.

## CHAPTER III

# SALLUST

IT IS in every way a wholesome thing that from time to time there should be a revaluation of the more notable figures in a country's literature, and it is only very few—Homer, Virgil, Shakespeare, Molière—whose preëminence has remained virtually unchallenged from generation to generation. Amongst the ancient writers of history only Thucydides comes near to being in that class, for certainly none of the Roman historians can be said to qualify. If popularity through the centuries is to be the test, Sallust is easily ahead of all his Roman rivals. The *Conspiracy of Catiline* and, to a less extent, the *War with Jugurtha* were widely read in the Middle Ages. How should they not have been when the high authority of St. Jerome had dubbed their author "most reliable" (*certissimus*)?[1] Extant manuscripts are numerous, and so are those recorded in the catalogues of medieval libraries, although few of these are likely to have been as well stocked as Christ Church, Canterbury.[2] The catalogue of *ca.* 1170 lists no fewer than eight copies of Sallustius. Three hundred years later, in 1470, the *editio princeps* of our author was printed at Venice, and from then on editions of the two monographs appeared in rapid succession. At the same time, a more critical attitude toward these works developed. The manuscripts of the later medieval period had become increasingly corrupt, and successive editors strove to provide their readers with a more accurate text. Indeed, as early as the middle of the ninth century the learned Servatus Lupus lamented the bad state of his copy and was anxious to obtain better manuscripts of both works for purposes of comparison and collation.[3] From the sixteenth century onward, editors also paid more attention to elucidating the

---

[1] For notes to chapter iii, see pages 169–172.

subject matter. Much of this earlier editorial material is included in the truly remarkable edition, published in 1710, by the Cambridge scholar, Joseph Wasse, a Fellow of Queen's College and private chaplain to the Marquess of Kent. Wasse himself consulted numerous manuscripts and added much material to illustrate the language and thought of Sallust, drawn from the whole range of Greek and Latin literature and even from the earlier Patristic authors. Thus there was justification for the saying attributed to Richard Bentley, "When I die, Wasse will be the most learned man in England." Thomas Hardy's Spirit Ironic would have chuckled at the fact that Wasse predeceased the tough old master of Trinity by four years!

That Sallust's narrative was sometimes at variance with other ancient sources treating the same events did not escape the notice of these editors. Wasse, for example, added a short appendix to the *Catiline* in which he dwelt on the discrepancies between Sallust's and Cicero's accounts of the conspiracy. There is something of eighteenth-century pomp in the title of this excursus, "Corollarium de Sallustio quaedam dissimulante in Catilinae historia." Still, neither Sallust's popularity as an author read in schools nor his reputation as an authority was seriously weakened before the closing years of the nineteenth century. The researches of John and particularly of Eduard Schwartz inaugurated a new era of Sallustian studies. His position as a stylist and a man of letters, who exerted some influence on Tacitus amongst others, remained unassailable, but his right to be regarded as a critical historian was seriously undermined. To this revised estimate of Sallust, which I believe to be essentially true, there has been a strong reaction, mainly in Germany, during the past two decades. The new interpretation reaches its extremest form in a monograph by Werner Schur, who sees in Sallust a philosophical historian deeply influenced by, though in some respects independent of, Posidonius. Schur, in common with a number of other scholars, even accepts as genuine the two *Suasoriae* or open letters addressed to Caesar and preserved in a Vatican manuscript (Vat. lat. 3864). He uses them as evidence to show what he believes to have been Sallust's gradual but consistent evolution as a thinker.[4] The Sallust who thus emerges in the pages of Schur and indeed of many of his German contemporaries is not, as Schwartz had argued, a writer who to the end remained a bitter political partisan, composing all his works in the interests of a political faction, but one who shed his party bias to become in the end a dispassionate, if pessimistic, critic strongly tinged with the Stoic doctrine as it was understood in the late Republican age. The difference between these two opposing views is not negligible. Clearly, if this most recent estimate of Sallust were correct, his stature as a historian would equal his merits as a literary artist.

Little enough is known of his life. Born in 87 B.C. in Amiternum, he came, like Marius and Cicero, from the Sabine hill country. His education seems to have been the best then obtainable and, although he did not, like many young Romans, go to Greece for the last part of his training, it included a sound knowledge of Greek literature.[5] Besides Thucydides, whose brevity he strove to reproduce in Latin and whose pregnant thoughts and descriptions he at times reëchoes,[6] Sallust shows acquaintance with Demosthenes' *Olynthiac Orations* and *De corona,* Plato's *Seventh Epistle* and *Menexenus,* and Xenophon's *Cyropaedia, Memorabilia, Agesilaus,* and *Anabasis.*[7] That his reading in Greek orators extended to the discourses of Isocrates is not only antecedently probable, but is borne out by specific passages.[8] At the same time, as we shall see, many of the *sententiae* in Sallust, so far from proving his originality, were by his time commonplaces alike of rhetoricians and philosophers. Of later Greek writers he was certainly familiar with Polybius and Posidonius.

He began his public career with the quaestorship, though in what year is uncertain. In 52 he was one of the tribunes. Two years later he was expelled from the senate by censorial action, apparently because of complicity of some sort in the riots that followed Clodius' murder by Milo's gangsters. Scandal too had been busy a few years earlier with an intrigue between Sallust and Milo's wife, from which he emerged sore in body and with lightened purse. With Caesar in power at Rome, he was allowed to reënter the senate and became quaestor for the second time. Thanks also to the dictator's influence he was chosen to be one of the praetors for 47 and was sent to govern Juba's old territory, now annexed as the province of Africa nova. On his return Sallust was accused of extortion, but acquitted by Caesar; nevertheless he made no further effort to continue his public career, but retired into private life. Thus from 46 to his death in 35 he composed his historical works amidst the comforts and indeed luxury of his house on the Pincian, whose gardens were one of the sights of the capital. Neither his public nor his private life to 46 accords very well with the high moral tone which runs like a *Leitmotiv* through all his books. The probity of the reformed burglar who has turned policeman is always a little suspect!

The precise dates at which Sallust brought out his three works are uncertain, but there seems to be no reasonable doubt about the order of their appearance. The account of the Catilinarian conspiracy came first, and this was probably not composed until after the establishment of the Second Triumvirate in the autumn of 43.° The *Bellum Iugurthinum* may, then, have appeared about 40 B.C., and the *Histories* between that date and the author's death five years later. Sallust himself relates that, after deciding to retire from official duties, he was unwilling to pass his time in farming or hunting. Instead, he took up a plan that he had abandoned when he entered on the *cursus honorum,* and set himself to write Roman history *carptim,* that is to say, picking particular and self-contained topics which seemed to him specially significant. This description applies equally well to the *Bellum Iugurthinum.* He also assures his readers that he will be as truthful as possible and that he is free from the bias of political party. The same sentiment in different words reappears at the beginning of the *Histories*.[10]

The *Conspiracy of Catiline,* then, begins on a strongly personal note. Sallust had become disgusted with public life and had turned to the writing of history. He chose the conspiracy as his theme because both its criminal character and the danger that it brought on the state were highly remarkable. After a chapter devoted to Catiline's early career, he deviates once more to sketch very rapidly certain features of earlier Roman history, and especially to point out the growing corruption that had overtaken the body politic after Rome's final defeat of Carthage and her emergence as the leading power in the Mediterranean. Then, beginning with chapter 14, Sallust concentrates on his main subject. The *Bellum Iugurthinum* also opens with prefatory remarks on mankind and on the value of historical composition. Moreover, it was at the time of this war that the unfettered control of the government by the Roman nobility was first seriously challenged, and a long era of civil dissension and unrest began. After these preliminary chapters Sallust traces the youthful career of Jugurtha and the dynastic wars from which he emerged the victor. The war with Rome is then related in greater detail, though with serious omissions, and the monograph ends rather abruptly with the capture of Jugurtha and a brief reference to Marius' election as consul for 104 and his appointment to proceed as commander-in-chief to Gaul.

All that survives of the *Histories* is five set speeches, two letters, and numerous fragments, most of them very short, from the narrative portions. Even so, the total remains of Sallust's most ambitious work are sufficient to show its general plan and scope and to arouse keen regret that it is not one of the books that have survived unscathed from antiquity. Its plan was approximately this: After some introductory matter, the first Book narrated

the insurrection of Lepidus in Italy and the early stages of the
war against Sertorius (78–77 B.C.). Book II continued the Spanish War and described military operations in other areas—Asia
Minor, Macedonia, and Epirus. A good deal of space was also
assigned to political affairs in Rome (76–75 B.C.). The only long
fragment of narrative in this book deals with the operations of
Servilius at Isaura vetus and nova. In Book III, foreign affairs
include the war against the pirates in the western Mediterranean and off Crete, the first stage of the Third Mithridatic War,
and the final operations in Spain. On the home front the two
main episodes were the struggle between *optimates* and *populares* and the insurrection of Spartacus (74–72 B.C.). Two longish
fragments of narrative in this Book describe episodes in this slave
war. The fourth Book had two main topics, the operations of
Lucullus in Asia Minor and the political rivalries and party struggles at Rome which culminated in the election of Crassus and
Pompey as consuls for 70 (72–68 B.C.). The last Book continued
the campaigns of Lucullus in the Near East; it also gave an account of the passing of the Lex Gabinia and the concluding
phases of the war against the pirates (68–67 B.C.). All the narrative fragments in Books IV and V are regrettably brief. In several
of these Books, Sallust introduced geographical digressions—on
Pontus and the Black Sea, Crete, Sardinia, Italy and Sicily. In
so doing he continued a practice that he had already adopted in
the *Bellum Iugurthinum;* in this respect he was following the
prevailing fashion of Hellenistic historiography. Like Sisenna
before him, he appears to have broken away from traditional
methods; for, instead of arranging his material in strictly chronological order, he made some attempt to carry out a regional
grouping of events within a larger chronological framework.
Clearly, there was an advantage in keeping before the reader as
far as possible the interaction of party politics at Rome and foreign affairs; but the remains of the *Histories,* especially in the

later Books, are too scanty to allow us to judge how far Sallust succeeded in his aim.[11]

No ancient historian felt any obligation regularly to cite or even to indicate his authorities, and the introduction into the text of official documents was in general avoided for reasons of style. Sallust is more reticent than most; certainly he gives us much less information about his sources than either Livy or Tacitus. He praised Fannius, one of the annalists, for truthfulness, and the elder Cato for brevity, though finding fault with some of the Censor's interpretations.[12] Sisenna's book he regarded as the best treatment of the war years from 91 to 80 B.C., but thought him too favorable to Sulla.[13] Sallust must have been familiar with all three of these writers, even as he was with Posidonius and at least parts of Polybius. Rutilius Rufus makes several appearances as an officer serving in the war against Jugurtha. Sulla, of course, played a leading part in the final phases of the same campaign. Elsewhere there are frequent allusions to the *dominatio Sullae* which, according to Sallust, marked an important stage in the decline of public and private morality. But, although it is intrinsically probable that Sallust consulted the *Memoirs* of both these men, he nowhere gives a hint that he had done so. He introduced two letters in his account of the Catilinarian conspiracy; that from Catiline to Q. Catulus is probably the genuine document, but the communication from Manlius to Marcius Rex is not.[14] Suetonius avers that a grammarian, L. Ateius, compiled a compendium of history for Sallust's use, but it is hard to say whether this bit of gossip had any foundation in fact.[15] Although Sallust refers directly only to the *First Catilinarian Oration* of Cicero, he had presumably read the other three also. Finally he refers to rumors or gossip current in Rome and either expresses dissent or leaves the question of its truth undecided.[16] Two letters are inserted in the *Histories,* one from Pompey to the senate and one from Mithridates to the king of Parthia. Both have been subjects of controversy, but it is a mistake to regard either as a genuine historical document. It is likely enough that Pompey sent a strongly worded dispatch to the Roman government, complaining of lack of support in the Sertorian War; but the letter reproduced in the *Histories,* though it may give the gist of what Pompey wrote, has Sallustian features.[17] Mithridates' epistle is a rhetorical fiction and not without absurdity. Can we seriously believe that the king of Pontus, in order to win over Arsaces of Parthia as an active ally against Rome, would send him a historical disquisition on Roman imperialism? The keynote of the letter is Rome's *cupido profunda imperii et divitiarum.* Sallust, in short, is once again harping on the theme which recurs so often in his writings, the evil effects of power, ambition, and avarice on Rome and the Roman character. This to him is more important than historical accuracy or even probability.

The introductions in Sallust's works have been much admired even by those who admit that as a historical writer he is full of political bias. The recent school of German critics tends to regard them as a proof of a philosophic mind with a strong predilection for Stoicism. The fallacy in either case lies in the assumption that the thought expressed by Sallust is marked by originality. Unquestionably, the opening chapters in the *Catilina* and *Bellum Iugurthinum* are models of terse and even epigrammatic latinity, but for the most part the ideas there set down had long been the common property of the philosopher and the rhetorician. Thus, the concept that man differs from the other animals because he has a soul or mind to direct him had been formulated by Plato, Aristotle, and Isocrates, who also discusses the function of reason and therefore speech in man.[18] Reflection should precede action, says Sallust (*Cat.* 1.6). True enough; but the same sentiment was already a commonplace in the Attic orators. If men, we read in the beginning of the *Bellum Iugurthinum,* took as much trouble to win what is good as they do in hunting after things that are without value or even dangerous, they would master and not be mastered by Fortune. A similar estimate of the operation of chance in human affairs was placed by Herodotus in the mouth of Artabanus.[19] In all three of his works Sallust dwells on the topic of national degeneration; for example:

When the fear of Carthage had been removed and men had time to exploit their quarrels, numerous riots, disloyal factions, and finally civil wars ensued, while a few powerful individuals, on whom the majority had conferred their favor, under the honorable name of senate and plebs were aspiring to despotism. Citizens were called good and bad not to mark the character of their services to the commonwealth—for all alike were corrupt,—but men were reckoned good in proportion to their wealth and power to harm, inasmuch as they defended the existing conditions.

&#10022; &#10022; &#10022;

Since that time the manners of our forebears have not declined little by little, as was formerly the case, but have tumbled down headlong like a torrent. Young men have been so vitiated by luxury and greed that one may fairly say that a generation of men was born who were unable themselves to hold property or to allow others to do so.[20]

The good old days when valor, true patriotism on the part of the governing class and of the governed, in short, national and personal *virtus* prevailed have been followed by a century of greed, luxury, and self-interest. Sallust places the beginning of the decline in political and personal morality after the final defeat of Carthage, with a further declension dating from the age of Sulla. In stressing the change for the worse that set in after the *metus Punicus* had been lifted in 146 B.C. he may well be adopting the interpretation of Posidonius. So far one may agree with Schur and others. But we have already had occasion to note how two rival theories of human progress had been current for centuries in the Greek world. Idealization of the past, moreover, was a commonplace of Greek oratory, and so also was the duty of the state to promote ἀρετή in its citizens and to curb luxury and greed.[21] Even the contrast between the costly private dwellings of the writer's own time with the stately temples of old when the citizens lived in frugal simplicity had already been drawn in two familiar passages of Demosthenes.[22] No one disputes that the Punic Wars and the intervention of Rome in the world of the eastern Mediterranean had a profound effect on the political, economic, social, and intellectual life of Rome and Italy. The accumulation of wealth and the growth of refinement or even luxurious habits produced conditions incompatible with the simple manners and sterner code which were believed to have been characteristic of earlier centuries. Criticism of contemporary morals, especially of the young people, was already being voiced in Rome in the second century. The annalist Piso in a passage which Sallust may have imitated accuses the young generation of libertinism, and one of the longer fragments of Lucilius describes what is meant by *virtus*.[23] Whether this *degeneratio* from the *mos maiorum* set in during the age of the Gracchi, as Posidonius and Sallust maintained, or somewhat earlier, as Panaetius and Polybius apparently believed, is relatively unimportant. What matters is that Sallust and probably Posidonius also, so far from enunciating a new philosophy of history, were thinking about human experience on more or less traditional lines. In their attitude to Roman politics since the Gracchi, the two diverged. Posidonius appears to have been in general sympathy with the senatorial regime, even though his charge of growing corruption might involve individual members of the order. Sallust is consistently on the side of the *populares,* though he can be critical of their leaders. If he wrote according to his honest belief, he was more than a party pamphleteer. We do not so label Macaulay, who was nevertheless the apostle of the Whigs. It is particularly in the *Histories* that Sallust's interpretation ran directly counter to the one prevailing among the upper class of Romans. No contemporary histories composed from a pro-

senatorial point of view survive, but that such existed is clear
from traces in later authorities. Sallust's interpretation is certainly
vulnerable; for a reasonable case can be made out for the view
that the *nobiles* were not as uniformly black as he would have
us believe, and that Posidonius' account of the age of Marius and
Sulla was more trustworthy than his.[24]

In emphasizing the personalities of history Sallust is the forerunner of Tacitus and Suetonius, and this approach is obvious
in all his works. What the reader retains longest in his mind is
the pen pictures of Orestilla, Fulvia, Sempronia, Micipsa, and
Bocchus, and the characterizations, largely through the medium
of speeches, of Catiline, Caesar, Cato the younger, and Marius.
So also in the *Histories* Sertorius and Pompey confront each
other as hero and villain of the piece; but there are minor characters, like Metellus, Marcius Philippus, C. Aurelius Cotta, and
Licinius Macer, whose portraits are hardly less vivid. The antithesis in the characters of Sertorius and Pompey is overdrawn,
but the accepted estimate of Sertorius, which sees in him the one
disinterested leader among the *populares* of his day, is assuredly
sound.[25] The same cannot be said of the Sallustian Pompey. He
is represented as a selfish and ruthless military adventurer, aim-
ing at supreme power, who from his early youth had been flat-
tered by admirers willing to compare him and his achievement
to Alexander the Great and his meteoric career. If we reject this
portrait of Pompey, as we must, it is not because it conflicts
with the uncritical eulogies of Theophanes of Mytilene, traces of
which survive in Plutarch, but because it cannot be reconciled
with the sober contemporary evidence in the writings of Cicero.
Partly owing to genuine admiration, partly for political reasons,
he had lauded Pompey to the skies in 66 in a public speech. But
his more considered judgment can be found in his correspondence, especially in the letters to Atticus. He admired Pompey to
the end, but he was not blind to his faults, the chief of which

was vacillation, a weakness irreconcilable with a ruthless lust for power. No one now accepts Mommsen's characterization of Pompey as a mere drill sergeant and little better than a poltroon who missed his chance in 62 B.C.; but clearly Sallust's interpretation is also untenable, in view of Pompey's political conduct when he returned to Italy after his settlement of the Near East, and indeed for the next twelve years.

Sallust's *ethopoiia* is both brilliant and memorable; its weakness lies in the absence of light and shade. His personalities are graphically portrayed, but they are devoid of psychological subtlety. Their treatment reminds one of the "types" familiar in the New Comedy and its derivatives. Even Catiline's early life is passed over in silence beyond a general statement about its dissoluteness. But we know now that in his youth the future conspirator had served honorably under Pompey's father as a junior officer in the war between Rome and her allies. The identification of Catiline with the C. Sergius who was a member of the military *concilium* that enfranchised Spanish troops for their loyal service can be regarded as proved.[26] One of the severest criticisms leveled against Sallust by older critics like Schwartz was his deliberate hostility to Cicero. Attempts have been made more recently to defend the historian and to prove that he treated Cicero with reasonable impartiality;[27] but in either case the critics have tried to prove too much. Some of Schwartz's strictures were too severe, but certain facts about Sallust's narrative cannot be explained away. He has not given us a portrait of Cicero comparable to those of other leading figures concerned in the conspiracy and its suppression. He has distorted the facts, thereby detracting from the senior consul's achievement. The importance of the *Fourth Catilinarian Oration* to counteract the proposal of Caesar, and the skill with which Cicero indicated the course of action that should be taken without overtly abandoning the impartiality expected of a presiding officer, are still too often forgotten by those who describe this speech as weak compared with the three that preceded it. Sallust gives no hint of all this, since his one purpose is to represent the debate as a verbal duel between Caesar and Cato. Then, as though his admiration for both men were not already patent, he follows up his account of the meeting in the senate by a digression, his famous evaluation and comparison of these two public men. The summing-up of the character and actions of a statesman or military leader was nothing new. Thucydides had abandoned his usual objectivity when he gave his readers an estimate of Pericles and, more briefly, of Themistocles. Nor was it an innovation to juxtapose two or more eminent persons; for Polybius, when recording the deaths of Philopoimen and of Hannibal in the same year, had summed up the merits of these two and had added an appreciation of Hannibal's greatest antagonist, Scipio Africanus.[28] The novelty of Sallust's procedure lay in appraising side by side two men of different political parties and of opposite political ideals. In the eulogy of Cato we may perhaps also see the initial stage in the process by which in a generation or two he became an almost legendary figure, an actual example of the Stoic sage. Sallust achieved a brilliant piece of writing, but at the cost of his credit as a historical authority.

Descriptions of battles, sieges, and other military undertakings in Sallust, as in the majority of ancient historians, show a strong generic resemblance. Once more we have to reckon with the influence of the rhetorical schools in which declamations dealing with these topics were a regular feature of the curriculum. On the other hand, there were in actual fact similarities in the various actions in ancient warfare. The procedure followed by the assaulting forces and by the defenders in a siege, the tactical evolutions of the legions, even though at least since Marius' reforms they had been more mobile than most infantry units of antiquity, the means adopted for the protection of Roman encampments against hostile attack—each of these operations tended to conform to a standard pattern. There would be variations in detail due to local conditions, but few writers were either expert or well-informed or even interested enough to strive after accuracy of presentation; instead they were satisfied with a stock description with due emphasis on the dramatic and the pathetic. One need only compare the siege of Syracuse as told by Thucydides, though even he is not clear in every particular, with Livy's account of Marcellus' siege of the same city, in order to see the difference. Livy writes a spirited narrative, but it is full of difficulties because he has paid little attention either to the topography of Syracuse or to the strategic problem which Marcellus had to solve. Or again, anyone familiar with the siege of Alesia or the Ilerda campaign in the pages of Caesar is likely to regard most other ancient accounts of a siege or of the encirclement of one army by another as very amateurish. Sallust's descriptive powers were of a high order, but it is only here and there that he relates a military episode with individual traits. The account of the battle near Pistoia, which brought the Catilinarian insurrection in Italy to an end, has always seemed to me more convincing than that of any engagement described in the *Bellum Iugurthinum,* and one wonders whether Sallust at some time had conversed with one of the survivors. Similarly in the *Bellum Iugurthinum* the capture of a Numidian stronghold through the initiative of a private soldier has unusual features.[20] Sallust, whether his source was written or oral, has made the most of a dramatic episode, but his account is more than just another routine description of a surprise attack.

Certain weaknesses of Sallust as a historian have often been pointed out and therefore need no lengthy exposition, especially as some of them are characteristic of other ancient writers of history. His chronology is careless and confused. His topographical data in the *Bellum Iugurthinum* are inadequate, although his official sojourn in Africa must have given him the opportunity to gather more accurate information had he desired to do so. Whether the *Histories* showed any improvement in these two respects it is hard to determine from the surviving fragments. Possibly they did, for the author was not under the same temptation, as he was in composing his two monographs, to telescope events or to shift their chronological sequence. Yet the description of the operations at Isaura, which is cited below, though lively enough, cannot be wholly accurate.[30] In the *Catiline* the events of the year 66 are confused with those of the year following. The meeting of conspirators at the house of Laeca in the night of November 6–7 is described before the crucial meeting of the senate held on October 21. In the *Bellum Iugurthinum* the chronology of Micipsa's later years and the adoption of Jugurtha is notoriously inexact, and the narrative of Marius' campaigns after he had succeeded Metellus as commander-in-chief omits as much as it includes. Accuracy is subordinated to dramatic effect, truth is sacrificed for the sake of upholding a preconceived theory. Sallust's predominant interest is not in the African war or in an attempted revolution at Rome, but in the juxtaposition of leading personalities and in the contrast between the leaders of the optimate party and their opponents. Yet his German admirer, referring to the last part of the *Bellum Iugurthinum,* can write: "Und auch hier gestaltet er die Tatsachen selbstständig um, wo ihm dies im Sinne einer höheren Wahrheit wünschenswert erscheint."[31] It is a strange theory of historical writing which justifies the manipulation of evidence in the interests of a higher truth!

Sallust admired both Thucydides and Cato for the terseness of their diction. His own success in attaining a similar quality in his works is remarkable even though he does not invariably succeed in avoiding ambiguity or even obscurity. The *immortalis velocitas,* which Quintilian so much admired in Sallust, had its dangers.[32] These faults, like certain mannerisms—for instance, his archaisms and his excessive use of the historic infinitive,—are more than compensated by the vividness of his narrative and the rhetorical effectiveness of the speeches that he put in the mouth of his characters. The two passages from the *Histories* that follow will serve to illustrate his narrative style in its maturity. The one describes the reception of Metellus in a Spanish town, and the other is a substantial fragment from the account of Servilius' campaign in southwestern Asia Minor:

When Metellus after a year returned to southern Spain, he enjoyed the honor of being welcomed by crowds of both sexes who flocked from every quarter to meet him. The quaestor C. Urbinus and others, having ascertained his wishes, invited him to a banquet and courted him in a way that went far beyond what was seemly for a Roman and indeed for a mere mortal. His house had been decorated with hangings and ornaments and a stage had been built for a performance of actors. At the same time saffron had been sprinkled on the floor and other preparations customary in a world-famed temple were made. Furthermore, as Metellus took his seat, an image of Victory lowered by a beam placed a wreath on his head to the accompaniment of artificially produced thunder. As he approached, incense was scattered before him as though he were a god. As he reclined he was clad in an embroidered robe. The feast was of the choicest kind, and not only the length and breadth of the province but Mauretania across the sea had been ransacked for many kinds of fowl and game hitherto unknown. These events caused some lessening of his reputation, especially in the eyes of older men of simple habits (*sanctos*), in whose judgment this display was a mark of arrogance, offensive, and unworthy of the Roman rule.

⟡   ⟡   ⟡

Then at a sudden signal when it was already the time of the second watch the enemy attacked at the same instant from both sides. First, amid great confusion they hurled their spears without fixed aim through the darkness of the night. Later, when the Romans purposely replied neither with missiles nor battle cries, the enemy thought that they were paralyzed with fear or that their defense works had been abandoned; and so they rushed eagerly into the trenches, and those who were swiftest across the earthworks beyond. Then at last the Romans who were standing on top hurled rocks, spears, and wooden stakes and threw into confusion many who had almost made their way across, striking them at close quarters or in any way they could. A sudden panic seized the attacking force; some were transfixed on the ramparts, others were impaled on their own weapons, and the trenches were filled with the many fallen. The remainder found safety in flight from the uncertainty of the darkness and fear of ambush. After a few days shortage of water compelled surrender; the town was fired and its people sold into slavery. Under the influence of these horrors a delegation soon came from Isaura nova to sue for peace; they promised to give hostages and to carry out the Roman commands.

Servilius, being well aware of their fierce nature, and that not war weariness but sudden terror led them to ask for peace, as soon as he had come up to the city walls with his whole army, for the moment behaved to the delegates with complaisance, so that they should not change their mind about their errand, and observed that if all were present the surrender would be effected smoothly. Meantime he restrained his troops from looting the countryside and from doing any damage. The townsfolk voluntarily handed over grain and other supplies, and Servilius pitched his camp in the open plain so that they might have no ground for suspecting him. But later, when after the transfer according to orders of one hundred hostages a demand followed for the surrender of deserters, arms, and artillery, the younger townsmen, first according to plan and later as each found the right opportunity, with loud shouts began a riot all over the town, protesting all the while that as long as there was breath in their bodies they would refuse to give up either arms or allies. But the men who because of age were less pugnacious and old enough to have learned to the full the power of Rome were anxious for peace; yet the guilty knowledge of their crimes made them afraid that, once they had handed over their weapons, they would quickly suffer the extreme penalty of the vanquished. While these disorders and the turmoil of the whole citizenry crowding together to reach a common plan were at their height, Servilius judged that the surrender of the town was a forlorn hope save under the stimulus of fear. So without warning he seized the mountain sacred to the Great Mother Goddess which was within javelin-throw of the high ground in the town.[33]

The orations are essentially Sallustian, even where he makes some effort to imitate the manner, and thereby throw light on the character, of the speaker. This is perhaps most apparent in the speech of Cato the younger before the senate and in the long harangue of Marius to the Roman people.[34] Following a practice customary since Thucydides and also conformable to the teaching of the rhetorical schools, the speeches are commonly composed in pairs; but they were not, like the speeches of Caesar and Cato in the *Catiline,* always introduced together on the same historic occasion. In the *Histories,* Lepidus, the would-be revolutionary, and Philippus, the highly respected representative of the ruling class in Rome, are so contrasted, and there is a similar juxtaposition of personalities and points of view in the orations of the moderate and well-meaning Cotta and the fiery tribune, Licinius Macer, even though they are inserted in different Books.[35] It has indeed been maintained that in the oration of Philippus Sallust has entirely adopted the style of the speaker, or, as one critic would have it, "has abandoned his own diction and completely assimilated that of the speaker."[36] This is not true. Sallust certainly succeeds in reproducing certain characteristics of Philippus' oratory, as described by Cicero in the *Brutus,* but the Sallustian authorship is never in doubt. There are too many words and turns of phrase that are typical of the historian and can be paralleled in other passages of his works.

For the modern translator Sallust is a hard nut to crack. We have already noted the brevity of Caesar's *Commentaries,* but Sallust's narrative style is often even more compressed. Thus, in the passages quoted the number of English words is very greatly in excess of those in the original Latin, and much of its trenchancy is inevitably lost. This is true also of renderings into French, although that language is in some respects better adapted for reproducing Sallust's essential quality.[37] In the reflective passages the difference is even more marked. It is, of course, true that because Latin is a highly inflected language there will always be a certain disparity in the length of the original passage from a Latin writer and that of a modern translation; but the difference is more striking in writers like Sallust and Tacitus than it is, for example, in a Ciceronian passage.

Sallust, though he falls short of Tacitus in this respect, is also a master of the pithy maxim and the brief characterization. Thus he says of Jugurtha, "vivit tamen in avido ingenio pravom consilium"; on Cato his final judgment is, "esse quam videri bonus malebat; ita quominus petebat gloriam, eo magis illum sequebatur." What could be more biting than the seven words characterizing Pompey as Sallust saw him, "modestus ad alia omnia nisi ad dominationem"? Among the many brief *sententiae* we may recall the following: "Ita imperium semper ad optumum quemque a minus bono transfertur." This may be wrongheaded, but it is very neat. So also is his comment on warfare, "omne bellum sumi facile, ceterum aegerrume desinere." Polygamy as practiced by the Numidians calls forth a dry comment, which also suggests that the historian was not wholly devoid of humor: "Ita animus multitudine distrahitur; nulla pro socia optinet, pariter omnes viles sunt." Most familiar of all is the maxim, "concordia parvae res crescunt." It is the motto of one of the ancient guilds in the City of London and of its school for boys, founded in 1561 under the headmastership of the redoubtable Richard Mulcaster.

To sum up: Sallust's merits as an artist have obscured, or made his readers willing to forget, his faults. As a historical authority he is at best in the second rank. To exalt him above Livy or even to put him on an equality with Tacitus is only possible for a student who has not penetrated below the surface, or for a critic who starts out with a preconceived theory of his own and twists the facts into conformity with it. Yet Sallust's value to us is considerable, mainly because his writings contain an interpretation of

Roman history during the late Republic, often differing from that in our other sources and opposed to the optimate tradition. Even his speeches are valuable historically; for they are full of *ethos* and convey Sallust's estimate of the men in whose mouth he has placed them. The moralistic tone observable in portions of the *Catilina* and the *Bellum Iugurthinum* may have little appeal in our age; but it enlisted the sympathy of St. Augustine and was one of the reasons for the popularity of Sallust in the Middle Ages. Nor, in estimating his continued appeal, should we forget the novelistic quality of his two monographs. This has insured him many readers and not a few literary imitators.[38]

## CHAPTER IV

# LIVY, THE MAN AND THE WRITER

THE STUDENT who turns to the standard histories of Latin literature will find there the names of many late Republican and Augustan authors whose literary activity was at least partly devoted to historical writing of one sort or another. Contemporary history, either in annalistic form or in the more intimate and less objective shape of memoirs, predominated, but antiquarian research was not neglected. Even universal history for Latin readers found an exponent in Pompeius Trogus, just as his contemporary, Nicolaus of Damascus, attempted a new synthesis of Oriental, Greek, and Roman history for the Greek-speaking world. Nearly all these authors are little more than names to us. Fragments of their long-forgotten works are few, or else we know them only as we know Trogus—through the much-abbreviated versions of later compilers. And no one who has perused a writer like Justin is likely to gainsay Francis Bacon's acid comment: "As for the corruptions and moths of history, which are Epitomes, the use of them deserveth to be banished, as all men of sound judgment have confessed, as those that have fretted and corroded the sound bodies of many excellent histories, and wrought them into base and unprofitable dregs."[1] Trogus' *History,* if it were recoverable, might prove to be of some interest; but in the main it is open to question whether either history or literature is much the poorer for the loss of these various compositions. One exception to this generalization must be made: the disappearance of Asinius Pollio's narrative of the two decades from 61 to 42 B.C. is deplorable. Much of it was the account of an eyewitness and would have formed a valuable contrast to the existing evidence, especially perhaps Cicero's *Correspondence*. The surviving fragments are very few, but Pollio's book was consulted by Plutarch and Appian; and there is little doubt that it had been used by Livy. Even so, we know little enough about it. Pollio appears to have treated Brutus and Cassius in a fair-minded way, but he was critical of Caesar's *Commentaries* and, as we have seen, questioned the accuracy of his casualty figures. He was throughout bitterly hostile (*infestissimus*) to Cicero. That was to be expected of a man who was a partisan of Mark Antony.[2]

It would be instructive to know which of the annalists members of the reading public, who had no desire to make comparisons or researches but merely wanted a general account of Roman history, were accustomed to consult during the last decades of the Republic. It may well have been Valerius of Antium, whose often criticized work seems to have retained some authority for a century or more after his time.[3] Nevertheless there was room for a new treatment of the subject when Livy began his undertaking; and it is a fair deduction from the character and frequency of his allusions to Valerius that he deliberately aimed at providing his countrymen with a more sober and trustworthy version of their history than his predecessor had done.[4] That he read and used him together with other annalists cannot fairly be held against Livy, for it is a purely gratuitous assumption that Valerius was in every respect unreliable. He had certain weaknesses of which Livy was well aware, such as a tendency to exaggeration and perhaps to overdramatize his narrative; and he may have had a certain liking for scandal even when the evidence was slight.[5] These are grave faults, but they do not exclude the possibility that much of Valerius' narrative was reasonably accurate.[6]

Titus Livius was born in 59 B.C., the year of Caesar's first consulship. When he was ten years old his native town of Patavium became a municipality of Roman burgesses. But his family, in view of their gentile name, are likely to have attained the citizenship at some earlier date; for the Patavians enfranchised in 49 were enrolled in the *gens Fabia*. Patavium, or Padua, in the Venetic territory and a city of respectable antiquity, during the Augustan age boasted of no fewer than five hundred citizens wealthy enough to belong to the equestrian class. The townsfolk owed their prosperity to their fertile soil, their rich meadowlands, and their trade in wool and textiles of high quality.[7] Something of local patriotism shines through Livy's narrative when he says that this corner of Italy alone withstood the Gauls successfully in 387, and when he relates the abortive descent on Italy made by Cleonymus of Sparta in the year 302 B.C.[8] The men of Padua played a notable part in bringing final disaster on this Greek invader and his expeditionary force. Livy concludes his account as follows: "The prows of the ships and the spoils taken from the Laconians were set up in the old temple of Juno, and there are many Paduans still alive who have seen them. In memory of the naval engagement a ships' contest is held officially every year on the anniversary of the battle on the river which flows through the middle of the city." We wonder whether one of the "Paduans still alive" was a wide-eyed small boy destined to become Rome's greatest historian. Livy makes two other references to his native town. He alludes briefly and without comment to a civil disturbance at Padua in 174 B.C. which needed the intervention of a Roman consul, and he reports a story, repeated by Plutarch, from the period of the civil war. A certain C. Cornelius was an expert in augury and by that means astonished the townspeople of Padua: he announced on the day that the battle of Pharsalus was fought, first, that an engagement had been joined between Caesar and his opponents, and then, a little later, that Caesar had won. It is known from other sources that Patavium was Republican at that time and defied Antony and Pollio.[9]

We know virtually nothing about Livy's youth. Doubtless he received most of his earlier training in his native city; for there is no hint that his father imitated the father of Horace, who sent his boy to Rome because the local school at Venusia was full of young "toughs," the sons of tough centurions. The last part of his education Livy is likely to have received in Rome. Pollio subsequently affected to detect traces of provincialism in Livy's writing; for the modern student to hunt for this "Patavinity" would be as rewarding as to search for Scotticisms in Macaulay. That Livy was thoroughly trained in rhetoric needs no special demonstration; his own writings are sufficient proof. There is also much that is attractive in the hypothesis that the excursus on Alexander the Great in the ninth Book of his *History* is a rhetorical exercise composed originally by Livy in his student days. Certainly the attentive reader cannot fail to be struck by the difference between this passage and Livy's other writing. Both in the flamboyancy of its style and the immaturity of much of the argument this digression contrasts greatly with Livy's later manner.[10] These chapters on Alexander strongly suggest some familiarity on Livy's part with Hellenistic historians other than Polybius and Posidonius; for the hostile tradition concerning Alexander, which he reproduces, had been characteristic of writers trained in the Peripatetic school. One may also wonder whether his decision to introduce this excursus into his *History* was not due to something more than the pride of a grown man in a youthful composition of unusual promise. He may have had a more serious purpose—to protest against an excessive admiration of Alexander in the Augustan age.

Livy's interest in philosophy, although the direct evidence for it is slight, deserves more attention than it has usually received. The younger Seneca in one of his *Epistles* observes that "Livy composed dialogues which belong at least as much to history as to philosophy, and books which dealt expressly (*ex professo*) with philosophy."[11] The *History* itself, however, seems to give evidence that his early preoccupation with philosophy left a permanent mark on Livy. The cumulative effect of various phrases and judgments, often slight enough if considered individually, suggests that he was an adherent of Stoicism as understood and taught in his day. The matter is so important for a proper understanding of his mind that it needs to be examined in some detail.

Perhaps no feature of his *History* has jarred more on modern readers than the solemn record of prodigies and supernatural occurrences scattered through its pages. The nineteenth-century rationalist and the advocate of "scientific" history in our own day will alike argue that Livy should have had no truck with such old wives' tales. Such a line of argument is fallacious in two ways. The auguries and *prodigia* set down in Livy were an integral part of Roman and Italian history. They were widely believed, and called forth official countermeasures by magistrates and military commanders. For the writer of Rome's national history to have excluded such matters would have been tantamount to omitting an essential part of the historical tradition. The critics of Livy may retort that he should at least have made clear his own skepticism toward these supposed miracles. That he did not do so outright was, I suggest, due to his conviction that there was room for such untoward manifestations in the order of the universe.

The one philosophical school to justify these beliefs and to fit them into its philosophical system was the Stoic, and Posidonius had progressed much farther along this mystical path than his predecessors. Two of Cicero's treatises afford some guidance here. In his book *On the Nature of the Gods* there is a remarkable passage which reproduces the views of Cleanthes, the second of the great Stoic teachers. Cicero's dialogue is divided into three sections. The chief speaker in the first presents the Epicurean argument; similarly, Books II and III are assigned respectively to the champions of Stoicism and of the New Academy. Near the beginning of the second Book, Cotta elaborates four main reasons for believing in the existence of the gods. The third of these is the awe or fear inspired in human beings by lightning, storms, pestilence, earthquakes, showers of stones, raindrops like blood, landslides, unnatural offspring of man or beast, and so on; in short, everything that could be classed as *prodigia*. His list reads astonishingly like some of the longer catalogues of ill-omened occurrences in the pages of Livy. The other dialogue by Cicero which bears on this inquiry is the treatise *On Divination*. The chief speaker in the first part, Cicero's brother Quintus, defends the practice, and it is generally agreed that the substance of his argument is derived from Posidonius. In the second part Cicero in his own person demolishes the Stoic position, which to him seemed merely superstitious. Livy's own attitude seems to have been this: Like many Stoics, he is prepared to accept supernatural phenomena as part of the ordained order of things, but he is also fully aware that the reports of such manifestations may merely be the result of popular fear and idle rumor. "I leave the question undecided," he writes in one passage, "as also the statement that during the appeals to the gods to avenge the breach of treaties a storm burst from the sky with a terrific roar; for they may either be true or simply invented as an appropriate representation of the wrath of the gods." Or again: "Many portents were announced that year, and the more readily men of simple and pious mind believed in them, the more numerously were they reported." "As usual, no sooner was one portent announced, than reports of others were brought in." Yet a rumor that mice had nibbled gold objects in the temple of Jupiter at Cumae calls forth a testy comment: "Thus a perverted religious sense (*prava religio*) drags the gods into the most trifling events." There is also a remarkable passage which reads almost as if the historian had

been criticized by his contemporaries and felt it needful to justify himself. "I am well aware," he observes, "that through the
same disregard of religion, owing to which men of the present
day generally believe that the gods never give portents of any
future events, no prodigies are now reported to the government
or recorded in histories. But for my part, while I am writing
the history of olden times, my sentiments, I know not how,
become antique; and a kind of religious awe prevents me from
considering events which men of those days renowned for wisdom judged deserving of the attention of the state, and of
public expiation, unworthy of being recorded in my history."[112]
Epicureans and Skeptics alike rejected, though for different
reasons, what Livy here would defend. His general frame of
mind is surely in harmony with Cotta's argument in Cicero's
treatise: "For he who knows the causes of future events necessarily knows what every future event will be. But since such
knowledge is possible only to a god, it is left to man to presage
the future by means of certain signs which indicate what will
follow them. Things which are to be do not spring suddenly
into existence, but the evolution of time is like the uncoiling
of a hawser: it creates nothing new and only unfolds each event
in its order."[113]

One naturally turns to Livy to see how far his phraseology
or his general concepts support the hypothesis that he was a
convinced Stoic. The evidence is not as unequivocal as one
could wish, because two reservations must be made at the out-
set: it is unsafe to attribute to Livy himself Stoic sentiments
expressed by the characters in whose mouth he places speeches;
and there are concepts which, though conformable with Stoic
teaching, had long since become part of the common stock of
ideas taught in the schools of rhetoric. A good example of this
latter is the antithesis between the expedient (*utile*) and the
honorable (*honestum*) which occurs again and again directly or

by implication in Livy's speeches.[14] But Livy also uses the antithesis when, after contrasting varying opinions about Rome's policy toward the Greeks in 171 B.C., he adds: "the view of those senators prevailed who were more concerned with expediency than with honorable conduct."[15] Some caution is also needed in evaluating references in Livy to Fortune and to Fate or Destiny. The equivalent of our saying, "Fortune favors the brave," occurs in several forms; the adage itself was a commonplace. It is used with a wider application when applied to the statesmanship of Camillus, and is also found in conjunction with the notion of the mutability of Fortune.[16] Noteworthy, too, is a passage in which the concept of *Fortuna* seems to merge into that of Destiny. Livy, referring to an episode in the Third Macedonian War, adds the comment: "As neither commander was willing to attack, Fortune, which is mightier than human plans, brought about a conflict."[17] Allusions to *fatum* and its derivatives are less common and occur mainly in the first decade; for example: "But, as I believe, the fates were responsible for the birth of so mighty a city and with divine aid for the beginning of a mighty empire." Or again: "As fate was now pressing hard on the Roman city, the ambassadors, contrary to the law of nations, took up arms." Or again: "The young man was either impelled by anger or by shame at declining the contest or by the irresistible power of Destiny." And he comments on the family of the Claudii thus: "A dispute arose through that family which seemed marked out by Destiny to quarrel with the tribunes and the plebs." Less significant, since they concern quasi-mythical personages, are Hercules fulfilling the decrees of Fate and Romulus guided by the Fates.[18] Isolated, such phrases may seem ordinary; taken together and in association with other pointers in the same direction, they may imply a Stoic approach to life and to history.

Again, it is legitimate to ask whether it is mere accident that Livy's chief admiration is reserved for men like Camillus,

Aemilius Paullus, whose *abstinentia* is praised when he could have enriched himself by his conquests, Q. Fabius Maximus, and Scipio Africanus. In the Stoic ethics the four cardinal virtues were prudence or practical wisdom (φρόνησις), courage (ἀνδρεία), justice (δικαιοσύνη), and temperance or self-restraint (σωφροσύνη). In all four men some, if not all, of these good qualities were developed to an unusual degree; all four, in short, had at least some of the characteristics of the Stoic *sapiens*. But here again one must admit that other philosophical schools and even the rhetoricians taught the same ethical doctrine. In his account of the second century B.C. Livy gave great prominence to the character of Cato the Censor. But his admiration for him was qualified, and he contrasted him, in connection with the dispute in senatorial circles about the proper treatment of Carthage, with the advocate of moderation, Scipio Nasica. Cato was indeed a most expert politician (*sapientissimus in civitate*), but Nasica is a *vir optimus*. The emphasis on the highest type of ethical conduct is unmistakable.[19] Perhaps most significant of all, however, is Livy's famous estimate of Cicero, which followed his account of the orator's murder by the emissaries of the Triumvirs. The whole passage is so vivid—we owe its preservation to the elder Seneca—that it deserves to be quoted in full:

On the approach of the Triumvirs, Marcus Cicero had withdrawn from Rome, convinced—and he was right—that he could no more escape from Antony than Cassius and Brutus were able to escape from Octavian. First he fled to his Tusculan villa; then by cross-country routes he made his way to his house at Formiae, with the intention of sailing from Caieta. Several times he reached the open sea; but what with the contrary winds that drove him back again, and his inability to endure the pitching and rolling of the ship as there was a heavy ground swell, escape and life itself at length filled him with disgust. He returned to his villa, which lay on higher ground little more than a mile from the sea, remarking: "Let me die in my homeland which I have often saved."

The fact is well attested that his slaves were ready to fight for him with courage and fidelity, but that he bade them set down his litter and, without interfering, let that come to pass which a cruel Fate made unavoidable. His head was severed from his body, as he leaned out of his litter and without flinching offered his neck to his enemies. Yet this did not satisfy the brutal savagery of the soldiers. They cut off his hands too, as they reviled them for having written against Antony. The head was brought to Antony and by his orders was set up between the two hands on the Rostra, the very place where as consul, where many times as senator of consular rank, where in that very year against Antony, men had heard him speak and had been filled with wonder at his eloquence far surpassing that of any other man. The people could scarcely raise their tear-filled eyes to gaze at the mangled remains of their fellow citizen.

He lived sixty-three years, so that, even if he had not met his end by violence, his death would hardly be thought premature. His genius was fortunate in his works and in the rewards that they brought him. He himself enjoyed good fortune for many years; but in the midst of long-enduring happiness he at times was struck down by grievous wounds—his exile; the ruin of the party that he had championed; the death of his daughter, whose end was both tragic and cruel. He bore none of his misfortunes as a man should, save only his death. Yet to a discerning judge this might have seemed not wholly undeserved, because he had suffered at the hands of a victorious foe a fate no more cruel than he would himself have exacted, had the same good fortune been his. Whoever weighs his faults in the balance with his virtues will judge him a great man, a keen and notable personality, whose praise it would need a Cicero to extol.[20]

Livy's concluding estimate is indubitably Stoic in tone. He is full of admiration for the orator, but the man does not measure up to his exacting standard. The true Stoic will regard all misfortunes as indifferent (ἀδιάφορα) and will rise superior to them. It is the Stoic yardstick by which Livy measures Cicero. Would that we had Livy's extended estimate of the younger Cato; as it is, only one sentence has survived. His glory, says Livy, with reference to Cicero's eulogy of Cato, and Caesar's attack on him, could neither be enhanced by praise nor diminished by blame. In short, it is evident that the historian contributed sensibly to that virtual apotheosis of Cato which is familiar to readers of Lucan and Tacitus.

The famous preface to the *History,* if it does not strengthen our hypothesis, contains nothing that is at variance with it. Both the love for the past and the pessimism about the present are neither peculiar to, nor incompatible with, Stoicism. The notion that the value of studying the past resides in the guidance it affords for present and future conduct Livy shares with Thucydides, Polybius, and others. In the *History* itself he in general keeps his personality in the background, and this reticence makes the revelation of his mind and purpose in the preface all the more precious.

Whether my undertaking will be worth the labor spent on it, if I record the achievements of the Roman people from the foundation of the city, I am not quite sure, nor, if I were, should I venture to say so; for I see that it is a task at once old and often tried, while new writers all the time fancy that they will offer in respect to the facts more reliable information, or in their style will improve on the uncouthness of the ancients. However that may be, I at any rate shall be content myself to have furthered, as far as in me lies, the remembrance of what the foremost people on earth have achieved; and if in so great a crowd of historians my own repute were dim, I should take comfort in the renown and eminence of those who will eclipse my fame. Besides, the subject brings with it immense toil, seeing that it reaches back more than seven hundred years and, starting from small beginnings, has grown so much that it is now burdened by its very magnitude.

I do not doubt that most readers will take less pleasure in the earliest period and that which immediately succeeded, as they make haste to reach those recent events through which the strength of a people long dominant is exhausting itself. I, on the other hand, shall also seek this reward for my toil—to turn away from the sight of the troubles which our age has looked upon for so many years, at least for as long as I am working over those olden times with close attention, free from every uneasiness of mind that, though it could not make the historian swerve from the truth, might yet disturb him.

It is not my intention either to affirm or to disprove the traditions about events that happened before the city was founded or its founding was planned. Their place is more properly in epic poetry than in the authentic record of history. So much licence we concede to antiquity, by mingling human agency with divine to render the foundation stories of cities more venerable; and, if any people ought to be allowed to treat its origins as sacred and trace them back to divine authorship, it is the Romans, whose fame in war is such that, when they choose to put forward Mars as their sire and the sire of their founder, the nations of the world accept the claim as calmly as they accept our sovereignty. Still, whatever criticisms or opinions shall be expressed about these and like questions, I shall hold them of small account. Rather I would have every reader focus his mind sharply on these topics: the life and manners of the Romans; by whose agency and by what policies in peace and war they acquired and enlarged their dominion. Then, as discipline relaxed little by little, let him follow in his mind the national character which at first declined slowly, then sank more and more, and at last began to tumble headlong into ruin, until he arrives at our present age when we can bear neither our vices nor their cures.

There is this wholesome and fruitful advantage above all in an understanding of the past, that you look upon examples of every type set out on a conspicuous monument. From them you may take for yourself and for your country what is worthy of imitation, and what you may avoid because it is base in origin and base in its outcome. And yet, unless love for my undertaking deceives me, there has never been a commonwealth greater or more high-principled or richer in good examples; nor a state into which luxury and greed have made their way so late, nor one in which poverty and thrift have been held in such high honor and for so long a time—in short, the less the wealth, the less it was desired. Of late, riches have brought avarice in their train; and profusion of pleasures, the craving through luxury and lust to ruin oneself and to destroy everything.

But complaints, which even when perhaps called for will be distasteful, must assuredly have no place at the beginning of this great undertaking. Rather should we begin, if it were customary for us writers of history as it is for poets, with good omens and vows and prayers to the gods and goddesses that they grant a happy outcome to the heavy task that we have begun.

Let us now turn to the *History* itself. When completed, it comprised one hundred and forty-two Books, or rather rolls of parchment or papyrus, which contained a great deal less than would a modern printed book. A rough calculation suggests that the entire *History* would have filled some twenty-four or twenty-five crown-octavo volumes of three hundred pages each. Livy took approximately forty years to carry out his great undertaking, so that, on an average, he composed the equivalent of some two hundred pages of print every year. This is a very substantial amount, but it is absurd to argue that such a rate of progress precluded any extensive study of earlier writers.[21] We must, moreover, take into account also the preparatory years before Livy began the actual composition of the *History*. There is little internal evidence, but it is certain that the first decade was not finished until after 27 B.C. Book XXVIII was composed after 19 B.C., and the lost Book LIX contained a reference to a law of 18 B.C.[22] If the first five Books were completed fairly soon after 27 B.C., we may assume that Livy was about thirty or slightly older when he started to write. What, then, of the previous years of his life? It is reasonable to assume that he had formulated his great project long before and that the years between twenty and thirty were expended on preliminary studies. We shall never know his method of work exactly; but we can be sure that he had a retentive memory, for its training was an essential part of ancient education. Nor should one exaggerate the physical difficulties that confronted him. Manuscripts of earlier historians may have been rather scarce, and the ancient roll was certainly less easy to read and to handle than the later codex or modern book; still, these drawbacks would have been largely overcome in the long period of preparation that we are justified in assuming Livy to have gone through.[23] He would naturally continue his reading and research while the work was in course of composition; but the essential point is surely that his mind was already well stocked when he began to write. The *History* was a big undertaking, but not as stupendous as some would have us believe. The library edition of Macaulay's collected works fills twelve stout volumes. Yet Macaulay during most of his adult life was busy with public affairs and died at the age of 59. Alison's *History of Europe from 1789 to 1815* filled ten volumes and appeared between 1833 and 1849, and he too was not solely occupied with authorship. The division of the Books into sets of ten was not made by Livy, but has some justification. Thus he begins Book XXI with a special preface in which he draws attention to the unique nature of the Hannibalic War. Book XXXI, again, opens with an introduction of some length. There Livy lays stress on the magnitude of the task completed and on the even more formidable task that still lies before him. It is probable that similar forewords occurred from time to time in the lost portions of the *History;* indeed, the elder Pliny refers specifically to such a preface.

The picture which too many modern critics persist in drawing of Livy makes him a superficial hack who always follows one predecessor and occasionally adds bits from one or two other authors. Such foolish assertions are surprisingly difficult to quash, being repeated from text to text and handbook to handbook. But Livy was a great artist and his *History* was a very great work of art, which could not have been created by a botcher working at haphazard. Nor was his handling of sources, as I shall attempt to show in the next chapter, as uncritical and superficial as it has often been represented. Less than a quarter of the *History* has survived; yet, by using the summaries of the lost Books, it is possible to estimate with some accuracy the scale on which it was composed. The early period of Roman history, as was to be expected, was described with relative brevity; for the first decade covers a period of about four and a half centuries. In the lost second decade the treatment was already much fuller—ten Books to portray the events of seventy-four years. The third decade, dealing with the age of the second war with Carthage, covered the history of only eighteen years. For the second century B.C. the scale appears to have been rather uniformly ten Books to twenty-four or twenty-five years. But when Livy reached the troubled years of the declining Republic, the average works out exactly as a Book a year.[24] Livy ended his narrative with the death of the elder Drusus in 9 B.C., but the twenty-two years from 30 to 9 B.C. were compressed into nine Books. To judge by the brief summaries, these latest Books were not longer than the average. The epitomes also reveal another interesting fact—that these Books, from CXXXII to CXLII, were mainly concerned with the campaigns through which the Roman frontier was advanced to the Danube and for a time beyond the Rhine almost to the line of the Elbe. How are we to account for this sketchy and one-sided picture of the Augustan principate? One obvious reason may have been that, by the time that he reached the final section of his *History*, Livy was an elderly man; another, that campaigns and military affairs were a leading topic in all histories written in antiquity. Nor can one doubt that Livy realized full well the outstanding significance of Drusus' and Tiberius' campaigns which extended the *imperium Romanum* and Roman civilization over a vast geographical area. Even so, it is also likely that he felt it more discreet to touch only lightly on, or even pass over in silence, the internal reforms of the emperor and the process by which the older form of Roman government was gradually transformed into a disguised despotism with which the historian was not wholly in sympathy. One may regret his decision, but, on the other hand, may commend him for his apparent neglect of those *chroniques scandaleuses* that drag their sordid and wearisome length through the pages of later writers. The tradition that he was sympathetic to the Republican regime rests on the sole authority of Tacitus, who makes two significant comments: Livy admired Pompey so greatly that the emperor dubbed him a Pompeian; and he treated prominent Romans of past ages with respect, even Brutus and Cassius, instead of reviling them as it was then fashionable to do.

Livy's original plan may have been to carry his *History* down to the death of Augustus, an event which he himself only survived by three years. Death may have overtaken him before he could complete his undertaking, or he may have abandoned it some time before. The elder Pliny makes a revealing comment when he says: "I confess my surprise that Titus Livius, the famous author, in one volume of his *History* begins with the remark that he now had won fame enough and could have taken his ease, did not his restless mind thrive on work."[26] So perhaps, as his *History* grew and grew, Livy did at times weary of it. Yet he was the type of man, not rare among writers and scholars, in whom the inner urge to compose creatively or to pursue investigations exerts an overmastering power to the end.

In the lost Books he dealt with a century and a half of events that had a revolutionary effect on Rome and the Empire. It will be convenient at this point to consider the scanty fragments together with the epitomes, so as to gain a general notion of the arrangement and of the author's point of view. Military history preponderated. The Third Punic War and the contemporary wars in the Near East, the campaigns of Marius, the four-year struggle between Rome and her Italian allies, the Mithridatic Wars, and Caesar's conquest of Gaul were all seemingly related in considerable detail. But the most elaborate treatment was reserved for the first and second Civil Wars. The internal affairs of Rome in the later Republican period and constitutional questions were not indeed overlooked, but Livy appears to have disposed of them with some brevity. It may be that the impression formed by a perusal of the epitomes is misleading and that these matters received fuller consideration in the actual *History* than the summaries suggest. But it is also possible, and in my opinion much more likely, that Livy intentionally avoided full discussion of the legislation and controversial questions of the first century. From one point of view they were perhaps dead issues; regarded from another, their detailed analysis might have led the historian onto dangerous ground.

Like other ancient historians Livy was deeply interested in personalities, that is to say, in the leading military and political figures. Here too the fragments and epitomes are not without value. His sympathies in general were with the senatorial government, in spite of its many faults. He was unsympathetic to Tiberius Gracchus and frankly hostile to Gaius. He admired the military genius of Marius and recorded that even Marius' opponents in the senate admitted that he had saved the commonwealth at the time of the Germanic invasions into southern Gaul and northern Italy. But he blamed Marius for the civil disturbances in 100 B.C. and implied that his sixth consulship had only been secured by wholesale bribery of the electors. In his final summing-up of the man, Livy describes his character and conduct as timeserving and lacking in consistency: "homo varii et mutabilis ingenii consiliique semper secundum fortunam."[26] Is the Virgilian echo Livy's own, or must we credit it to the epitomist? The historian's opinion of the younger Livius Drusus was not high. He disapproved strongly of P. Sulpicius Rufus and, with more justification, of Cinna. Evidently an admirer of Sulla, he nevertheless passed on him a judgment as severe as any that we know him to have uttered: "When he had restored the commonwealth, he befouled a splendid victory by conduct more savage than any man had been guilty of before."[27] He appreciated the military gifts of Sertorius, but implied that toward the end of his life he became cruel and spendthrift. If the abbreviator is to be trusted, Livy defined the so-called First Triumvirate as a *conspiratio inter tres civitatis principes;* this judgment implies that his attitude was critical. We have already heard his estimate of Cicero and Cato the younger. The evidence does not justify one in saying that he was unfriendly to Julius Caesar. But that he set down the widely quoted remark about him, that it was an open question whether Caesar's birth was of greater benefit to the state than if he had never been born, at least suggests that his admiration for the dictator was not unqualified. Of all the characters, however, who played their part in the thirty years between Caesar's first consulship and Octavian's final triumph, there was only one, as it would seem, toward whom Livy was uncompromisingly hostile, and that was Mark Antony. His mastery was impotent, he carried a law by violence, he inflicted great wrongs on Caesar, he was cruel, he wantoned with Cleopatra, and he was misguided in undertaking a war against Parthia.[28] The primary reason for this string of accusations was not consideration for Antony's rival, Augustus, but genuine disapproval of Antony's indifference to constitutional forms and his willingness to sacrifice Roman interests in order to minister to the whims and salacity of an Eastern queen. And if Livy was indeed a Stoic, then Antony the man was in every respect the antithesis to the historian's ideal. Be that as it may, a brief analysis of the judgments that he passed on notable men proves the entire justice of the elder Seneca's appraisal. He called Livy "by nature the most impartial judge of all great characters."[29]

CHAPTER V

# LIVY, THE HISTORIAN

No ASPECT of Livy's *History* has received more attention than his use of earlier writers, and none has called forth more varied opinions. The conclusions reached by modern critics, moreover, are so often mutually contradictory or destructive that one is disposed to question the value of much that passes for scholarly investigation. Most arbitrary is the school of thought which makes it an axiom that Livy, and for that matter ancient historians generally, always followed one main predecessor and only here and there added items taken from other writers. Protests have occasionally been raised against this assumption, and especially against the common assertion that, when Livy refers to "authors," he means only one person and is using a Latin idiom whereby the plural is employed for the singular.[1] But bad habits die hard, and this highhanded method of reducing Livy's *History* to the level of "scissors-and-paste" work, and that of the poorest kind, still continues. Even so good a scholar as Klotz can propound a theory that, because Livy quotes Valerius Antias three times in the fourth decade and accepts his version in these places, it can be assumed with certainty that Valerius was his main source for Spanish events to the end of Book XXXVIII. Yet Livy also names Cato the Censor, the clear implication being that he prefers Cato's more cautious estimate to Valerius' exaggerated figures. Again, Klotz states that Livy cites Valerius first and Claudius Quadrigarius only in the second place. But there is a passage where the reverse is true. To explain away this awkward fact Klotz has recourse to a theory of additions inserted after the completion of the book! He also blandly ignores the fact that already in the third decade Claudius is mentioned first,

---

[1] For notes to chapter v, see pages 174–176.

with Valerius second and Piso third.[2] I have taken this specific instance to show the lengths to which even a reputable scholar is prepared to go in order to fit the body of facts into his Procrustes-bed of preconceived theory. The truth is that Livy was critical of Valerius from the beginning; if he refers to him more often in the fourth decade than before, the simplest explanation is that for this period he had fewer predecessors to consult. The *Annals* of Fabius Pictor, Piso, and Macer all stopped before the opening of the second century. Doubt has often been expressed whether Livy used Fabius directly; but, unless we are prepared delib-erately to charge Livy with untruth, this doubt is unjustified. Fabius is mentioned by name six times, and two of these passages are decisive proof for any reasonable inquirer. In one Livy ob-serves: "I find in Fabius, who is by far the earliest authority, that Coriolanus lived to old age." In the other he says: "Other authors give the loss on each side as many times greater, but I refuse to indulge in the idle exaggerations to which writers are far too much inclined, and, what is more, I am supported by the author-ity of Fabius, who was living during the war." In four out of the six passages he emphasizes the antiquity of Fabius as compared with that of the other annalists whom he habitually consulted. Besides, his dependence on this annalist and consequent accuracy in describing one of the early engagements in the Second Punic War can be indirectly demonstrated.[3]

Livy alludes to his sources with a frequency unusual among ancient historians. Besides his references to Fabius, he mentions Claudius Quadrigarius by name twelve times, Coelius Antipater eleven, Licinius Macer seven, and Piso six. Valerius Antias' name occurs on thirty-six occasions. Of Polybius, whose name appears half a dozen times, Livy had the highest opinion, though this fact also has been called in question.[4] There is no doubt that in the fourth and fifth decades Livy followed him closely for the his-tory of the Greek world. Polybius is also the ultimate source of much material in the third decade. Livy, however, did not there mention him by name, and critics are still sharply divided on the question whether he made direct use of Polybius, at least before Book XXIX. Finally, there are some isolated references to other authors.[5] Far more usual, however, especially in the early Books of the *History,* where Livy was dealing with the remote past, is his employment of general phrases such as "it is related," "they say," "authorities disagree," "the general opinion is," "it is probable," and so on. Indeed, the variety of expressions used is remarkable and is calculated to convey to the reader every shade of judgment—from virtual certainty to complete skepticism about recorded facts and traditions.[6] And yet, superior persons continue to call Livy uncritical. Surely these usages prove the very opposite; they show that he was aware of the shortcomings of his predecessors and the all but hopelessly confused state of knowledge about the earliest centuries of Roman history. His unwillingness to be dogmatic—an unforgivable sin in the eyes of a German professor—and his skepticism in the face of weak or contradictory evidence are the measure of his intellectual honesty. The matter is so important that it is worth while to illustrate by actual quotation Livy's awareness of the difficulties that confronted him, especially in regard to the history and traditions of early Rome. He strives to ascertain where the balance of probability lies when a matter is in dispute, and he is willing to tell his readers frankly if he thinks it insoluble. "The subject matter," he remarks in one place, "is enveloped in obscurity; partly from its great antiquity, like remote objects which are hardly discernible through the vastness of distance; partly owing to the fact that written records which form the only trustworthy memorials of events were in those times few and scanty, and even what did exist in the pontifical commentaries and public and private archives nearly all perished in the conflagration of the city."[7] We have already seen that the archaeological evidence points to a certain

degree of exaggeration on Livy's part regarding the physical destruction caused by the Gallic invasion. The passage quoted also
raises another problem. Is it true, as is commonly stated, that
Livy did not trouble to consult such official documents as were
available in his day? The fact that such records are not directly
introduced into the narrative proves nothing; for to have done
so would have been to offend against the artistic canons of antiquity, which required that the style of the *History* be uniform
and not marred by the introduction of official decrees, laws, and
similar material. And even Thucydides generally conformed to
this practice.[8] Livy admits that for the early treaty with Ardea
he relies on Licinius Macer; but he quotes from old laws more
than once.[9] He refers to a statue and inscribed base at Praeneste,
honoring the prowess of M. Anicius in 216 as commander of a
garrison at Casilinum. He also reproduces the text of a votive
inscription commemorating the achievements in Sardinia of the
elder Tiberius Gracchus. His interest in old custom and religious
rite led him to record, "in the very words in which they are
handed down," the regulations governing the act of *devotio.*[10]
His account of the Bacchanalian conspiracy, on the other hand,
though a breathlessly exciting narrative, cannot be satisfactorily
reconciled with the evidence provided by the extant *senatus con-
sultum*. Yet, although he did not always inform himself by reference to original documents, we are by no means entitled to assert
dogmatically that he never consulted such sources of information at all. Another passage proves Livy's awareness that family
archives might be most untrustworthy. "It is difficult," he writes,
"to decide which account or which authority to prefer. I believe
that the true history has been falsified by funeral orations and
lying inscriptions on the family busts, since each family appro-
priates to itself an imaginary record of noble deeds and official
distinctions. It is at all events owing to this cause that so much
confusion has been introduced into the record of private careers

and public events. There is no writer of those times now extant who was contemporary with the occurrences that he relates and whose authority, therefore, can be depended upon."[11] Thus writes the historian who has often been described as an uncritical compiler! Francis Bacon had a clearer notion of the difficulties facing a writer like Livy, though he does not mention him as an example. But, in contrasting the writing of contemporary history with that of events long past, he observes:

So again narrations and relations of actions, as the War of Peloponnesus, the Expedition of Cyrus Minor, the Conspiracy of Catiline, cannot but be more purely and exactly true than histories of times, because they may choose an argument comprehensible within the notice and instructions of the writer; whereas he that undertaketh the story of a time, especially of any length, cannot but meet with many blanks and spaces, which he must be forced to fill up out of his own wit and conjecture.[12]

Livy fortified his own "wit and conjecture" with another type of source when composing the first decade, namely, the epic of Ennius, and possibly some other poetical narratives of Rome's distant past.[13] Indeed, his recognition that traditions and folk memories are likely to contain a core of truth and to rest on a basis of historic fact is in some ways sounder than the complete skepticism of his modern detractors. The Greeks had in a similar way appealed to the authority of Homer, and even Thucydides was no exception.[14] Genuine traditions handed down orally from one generation to the next are after all very different from rumors and idle gossip which have their day and then drop out of circulation.

Livy well knew the difference. After explaining that Valerius Antias had related a rumor current in Rome in 190 B.C., he observes: "As I can find no other authority who relates this rumor, the story should not in my opinion be stated as a fact nor yet dismissed as an idle tale."[15] A striking passage on rumors in wartime and on armchair strategists is put by Livy in the mouth of Aemilius Paullus. There is a timeless quality about these observations which makes them appropriate in any age and not least in our own:[20]

Trust fully my dispatches to the senate and yourselves; beware by your credulity of fostering rumors for which no man shall appear responsible. For I have noted this as a common occurrence, especially in the present war, that no one is so scornful of hearsay that his spirit cannot be weakened.[21] In every circle and, i' faith, at every dinner table are people who lead armies into Macedonia, who know where camp should be pitched, what sites should be occupied by troops, the time and right pass for invading Macedonia, the place for storing supplies, the hour when to engage and when it is better policy to remain inactive. Indeed, such people not only decide a course of action, but whatever steps other than those that they have approved are taken become a ground for arraigning the consul as though he were on trial. These are serious obstacles to the men in charge; for not everyone is able to be as steadfast and unmoved in the face of adverse rumors as Q. Fabius was, who preferred to let his authority be reduced through the folly of the people, to managing the affairs of the state ill, though with a fair reputation. Citizens, I am not the man to believe that commanders should not receive advice. On the contrary, the man whose dispositions are the result of his judgments alone I regard as arrogant rather than sagacious. What, then, is the right course? First, generals should receive counsel from those who are farseeing and who have expert knowledge of military affairs and have learned from experience; secondly, from those who are present at the scene of action, who see the locality, the enemy, and the opportune moment, and who share the danger like fellow passengers in the same ship. And so, if any man thinks himself qualified in the war that I am about to conduct to give me advice beneficial to the state, let him accompany me to Macedonia and not refuse his aid to the commonwealth. I will provide him with ship, horse, tent, and even pay his expenses. And, if it is too much trouble to do this and he prefers the easy life of the city to the hardships of active service, he should not steer the ship from land. The city itself provides plenty of topics for conversation; let him confine his talkativeness to these and realize that we shall be content with the plans formed in camp.

Fundamentally, Livy's habit of mind was conservative. But it is not in accordance with the facts to regard it as static, or fair to accuse him of narrowly aristocratic sympathies. Those sections in the early Books that describe the protracted struggle of the plebs for political and economic equality with the patricians are faulty in detail and in part even imaginary and, in the strict sense, unhistorical. Nevertheless, in its essentials the over-all picture of constitutional development is true. Livy disapproves of extremists and agitators on either side. The conclusion that he draws and impresses on his readers is that the sharp and sometimes violent clashes between the leading men of two groups of citizens were ended time and again through the good sense and willingness to compromise of the citizen body as a whole. But in the third decade, too, Livy brings out the essential solidarity of the Roman people and indeed of a majority among their allies—a solidarity which more than any other single factor brought about the ultimate failure of Hannibal's purpose. "Let people scoff," he remarks in a noteworthy passage, "at the admirers of the good old times. If there existed a kingdom of wise men which philosophers dream of but have not known, I should not think that either its rulers could be men of firmer character or more restrained in their ambition for power or the mass of the people show a better disposition."[18] This is his eulogy of the Romans when the Second Punic War had run half its course, and is plain enough. But it has not been sufficiently observed that Livy also brings out the soundness of the Roman state and its political institutions by the method of contrast. It is surely no accident that he repeatedly draws attention to the political organization prevailing in the Greek cities of Italy and Sicily, which brings them to revolution or at least to the edge of it. In so doing he is not merely relating the events of the war and pointing out that the governing class were usually friendly to Rome and the mass of the people (*multitudo*) hostile or actively pro-Punic; his secondary purpose is to contrast the Roman genius for government and the Greek lack of it. This conclusion is reinforced by the manner in which he speaks of Greek states elsewhere.

There was never a dearth of tongues ready to stir up the people. This phenomenon, found in all free states but above all in Athens, where public speaking carries the greatest possible influence, derives its sustenance from the favor of the masses.... The Athenians carried on the war against Philip with dispatches and words, in which alone they are strong.

The Greeks are "a people more valiant in speech than in action." The consul Glabrio contrasts unfavorably the Greeks in Asia Minor and Syria, "the most contemptible race of men and born to be slaves," with the martial Thracians, Macedonians, and Illyrians.[19] And Livy indulges in a delicate piece of satire when he makes Aristaenus, the president of the Achaean League, in 198 chide his countrymen for their talkativeness outside the assembly and their silence in it:

Where are those rival sentiments, Achaeans, which make you almost come to blows when Philip and the Romans are mentioned at your dinner tables or at social meetings? Now in an assembly called for this specific purpose, after you have heard the arguments of representatives on both sides, when the magistrates bring the question before you and the herald calls for speakers, you have become dumb.[20]

Actually what Livy here makes a matter of reproach to the Achaeans is a common trait in human nature, as any member of a university faculty is well aware!

The third decade and even the lost Books show Livy's approval of what he regards as healthy constitutional evolution and his dislike of extremism. This fact invalidates the arguments of Soltau and others in their discussion of his sources in the first decade. They have argued that Livy is inclined to side with the plebs in certain episodes—for example, the passing of the Canuleian Law and of the Licinio-Sextian Rogations—because he is there following Licinius Macer, whose sympathies were popular. Elsewhere, they maintain, where his point of view seems to be more aristocratic or unfriendly to popular agitators, he relied on some other annalist like Aelius Tubero. Now, quite apart from the fact that the heavy reliance on these two predecessors rather than their occasional use is an unproved assumption, Livy, I believe, exercises an independent judgment. His critical attitude to the episodes of Maelius (iv.13 ff.) and Manlius (vi.14 ff.) is determined not by their political party, but by their personal conduct. They were agitators whose ultimate aim was the establishment of a personal autocracy. "This is a thing to be noted," says Livy, "in order that men may see how great and glorious deeds are not only deprived of all merit but made positively hateful by a loathsome craving for kingly power."[21] And surely nothing could be plainer than his comment on the good sense of the people which after a bitter class struggle asserted itself, a comment accompanied by a contrast between then and now:

The result of that election showed that the feelings aroused in the struggle for freedom and human worth (*dignitas*) are different from those that prevail when the contest is over and judgment is unbiased. The people elected only patricians as tribunes with consular powers, being satisfied with this, that the plebeians had been taken into account. Where could you now find in one man such moderation, equity, and high-mindedness as then characterized the whole people?[22]

The question of Livy's real attitude toward early party struggles and the passages quoted in that connection lead naturally to another topic of fundamental importance. What value is to be placed on Books I to X and on the reconstruction of early Roman history that they contain? We have seen that Livy was often critical of the annalists, and it is clear that he himself was more restrained than they in handling early legends and traditions. Everyone admits that the story cannot be accepted as it stands. There are repetitions and duplications both in the accounts of the struggle between the orders and of the external wars of Rome, whereby essentially the same set of events is related twice over and treated as two episodes occurring at different dates. There are also anachronisms, but Livy's critics have often gone too far in trying to prove their existence. It is probable, for example, that the centuriate organization did actually come into being in the sixth century, as Livy implies.[23] Still, even if all his shortcomings are fully admitted, is not Livy's picture true in its essential lines? Even such a qualified acceptance of this portrayal, the fundamental trait of which is the contrast between the solid excellence of the early centuries, with their *mos maiorum* and *mores antiqui,* and the degeneration of later times, has recently been under attack. Mr. Henry, in an eloquent presidential address delivered before the Classical Association of England and Wales, has impugned the whole tradition of early Rome as it is found in the pages of Livy.[24] That tradition had grown up gradually, and Mr. Henry would trace it back, through Sallust and Cicero, to the Stoics of the second century. "It is clear, then," he concludes, "that the Roman tradition upon which Augustus relied has no solid historical basis to support it. It was the product partly of Roman patriotism, partly of Greek philosophy, and we cannot trace it beyond the second century B.C. That the Romans of an earlier period had any higher moral standard than the Romans of the last two centuries of the Republic is but a pious opinion." Up to a point Mr. Henry's skepticism is justified. We have already seen that the tendency to exalt the remoter past at the expense of more recent times, and the theory of a progressive degeneration of society from primitive purity of manners and simplicity of life, were a part of the stock of ideas common to philosopher and rhetorician. But one cannot ignore the historical facts of Rome's political growth in Italy and the gradual evolution of an equitable form of government for her citizens.

After all, Rome did control two-thirds of Italy on the eve of her first war with Carthage, and the loyalty with which the great majority of her allies, many of them but lately her opponents, stood by her in the darkest days of the third century is surely convincing proof that her relations with other communities in Italy were based on a firm foundation of equity and good faith. Similarly, with the passing in 287 of the Hortensian Law, the interests of all her citizens were at last fairly safeguarded. There is no doubt, on the other hand, that in the second century the relations between Rome and the Italians steadily deteriorated and that Rome was chiefly to blame for this, until the patience of the allies finally gave out in 91 B.C. Again, the essential features of the struggle between patricians and plebs are true, however much the course of that long political and economic duel may have been clouded by legend or distorted by the family loyalties of certain annalists. Early documents are regrettably few, but what little evidence exists bears witness to the sound political sense of the Romans. The text of the treaty which regulated the relations between Rome and the other Latin communities when Rome joined the Latin Federation early in the fifth century still existed in Cicero's day. He also informs us that the Twelve Tables in direct terms acknowledged the sovereignty of the Roman people. A well-qualified foreign observer like Eratosthenes could find occasion to praise the political institutions of both Rome and Carthage.[25] It is also legitimate to doubt whether the interpretations of Roman history put forward by Cicero and Livy, after every allowance has been made for their literary eminence, would have been generally accepted, if they had had little or no basis in fact.[26] To assume the contrary is to credit the Romans with an unbelievable ignorance about their own past. And besides, it would surely be possible to bring forward a sufficiency of historical parallels from other countries and other ages to illustrate the alternation of greatness and decline. A philosophical interpretation of this in terms of *prisca virtus* and *degeneratio* would not alter the basic facts, however much it might be beside the mark and useless as an explanation. Thus it is after all more reasonable with the late Warde Fowler to call the story of Livy's first decade true, "not in our sense, scientifically, but artistically and imaginatively true."

No one will deny that there are serious weaknesses in Livy, though some of them are common to all Roman and most Greek historians. There are anachronisms. The events and institutions of early Rome are sometimes interpreted in the light of the more familiar history of the later Republic and of his own experience. On the other hand, it borders on the captious to criticize Livy because he called Hannibal's headquarters by the Roman term, *praetorium,* and spoke of the Samnite armies as organized in legions. What should he have done? Should he have hunted for a Punic word in the one case and an Oscan in the other? And is there any proof that the military organization of the Samnites was quite dissimilar to the Roman? May it not have been modeled on it?[27] Livy, although he directs attention to a chronological difficulty (xxvii.7.5), thereby showing his awareness of the problem, is often careless in this respect. His battle scenes tend to conform to type and his topographical data are often unreliable. His intense patriotism makes him unfair in some of his estimates of Rome's enemies. These are some of the obvious criticisms that can be leveled against him, and there is some truth in all of them; but they have sometimes been overstressed to the point of being unjust. The search for anachronisms can be carried to the point where it borders on the absurd, and the disagreement on many points that still exists among modern investigators should induce a more charitable attitude to the difficulties with which Livy had to contend when he undertook his tremendous task. The chronology of the Spanish campaigns during the Second Punic War is faulty because the reckoning of the Roman annalists has not been brought into complete harmony with Polybius' dating by Olympiads, which began in the middle of the year. Vague and sometimes inaccurate topography and a certain generic resemblance in the descriptions of military operations, except where he adhered closely to Polybius, are traits that we find in most ancient historians. Certainly he was no worse in this respect than Sallust or Tacitus. The charge that patriotism prevented him from dealing objectively with the enemies of Rome in the third and second centuries cannot be gainsaid, but again this failing is not peculiar to him or to the ancients. Polybius, whom it is the present fashion to extol to the skies, is grossly and notoriously unfair to the Aetolians. And, to take a modern instance, it is only within the last few decades that serious historians in the United States and in England respectively have laid aside their prejudices and succeeded in being fair to both sides in their accounts of the American Revolution.

What, then, is the secret of Livy's success? First of all, there is the impressive achievement of relating the story of Roman history through nearly eight centuries with intellectual integrity and at an unfalteringly sustained level of art. Next, he brought before his readers vividly the greatness of Rome's past in a way that none of his forerunners had attempted, or, if they did, had been able to approach. In the third place, he was equally successful in narrative and in the composition of speeches. What he accomplished in both respects deserves a little further consideration.

The speeches which are so strikingly a feature of the *History* have been variously judged in modern times. Their introduction, as we have seen, was an essential part of the art of historical writing as practiced in antiquity. To me it seems a travesty of the facts to allege that they always smack of the rhetorical schools and that the long gallery of historical portraits that they bring before us is really a collection of abstractions or dummies.[28] Scipio Africanus in Polybius is an abstraction, if you will, a conglomerate of all the virtues; in Livy he is a living, breathing human being. And, if Scipio is Livy's masterpiece in the portions of the *History* that have survived, his characterizations of Fabius Maximus, Cato the Censor, and Aemilius Paullus are not unworthy companions. In large part these portrayals are achieved by the use of speeches attributed to them by the historian. The speakers in the first decade are inevitably less individualized, but even they have personality; they are not mere lay figures. Following the usual practice, Livy does not insert orations actually delivered by historic personages. On the other hand, the speech of Cato on the Oppian Law as composed by Livy contains tricks of Cato's style which Livy has deliberately introduced; for instance, the use of several nouns in succession without a copula, and the use of nouns and verbs in pairs. The speeches in Livy, then, are his own, but they are never mere declamations. Their purpose is partly to bring before the reader as vividly as possible questions of policy, but still more to portray with the sharpness of a good etching the character and psychology of the speakers, who are usually persons of prominence in military or political affairs. The speeches commonly appear in pairs, and with few exceptions they belong to the deliberative type. In the powerfully moving pleas of Demetrius and of Perseus before their father, Philip V, the tone and arrangement, as befits the occasion, approach more nearly to the forensic style. The *genus demonstrativum* is represented by a few examples, such as the eulogy of Rome uttered by the Saguntines or the discourse of Aemilius Paullus.[29] This latter, one of the most moving passages in Latin literature, is in part a funeral oration on his sons. A recent classification would separate the speeches into two classes, those in which Livy allows all the principles of rhetoric full scope and those in which there is less attention to the balanced construction of the speech because he is following his source closely. The distinction is unconvincing, since it rests on only two examples, two orations in which Livy reproduces Polybius with such fidelity that the rhetorical structure is less careful than elsewhere. To base a far-reaching generalization on so few particular instances is hazardous in the extreme, the complete negation of sound method in research.[30]

A special interest attaches to the speech of Camillus (v.51 ff.), for it has been said that its spirit is Augustan and that it is worthy to be set side by side with a famous passage praising rural Italy in Virgil's *Georgics*. It has also been viewed as Livy's protest against the rumors current in his day that the capital of the Empire might be moved from Rome to the Near East.[31] It may be so, but the speech is perfectly consistent with Livy's portrayal of Camillus; indeed, it crystallizes all those qualities that had made this worthy of early Rome a leading statesman. The strongly religious tone of the oration may rest on a sound historical tradition about Camillus, while it also accords with Livy's general attitude to the religious institutions of archaic Rome. It is also fashionable to see traits of Augustus himself in Livy's portraits of eminent men, for example, Capitolinus and Camillus. The weakness of this kind of interpretation is always the same; it rests on an unproved and unprovable assumption. In this particular instance one may say that Livy is inclined to idealize Rome's remoter past. He may have hoped that some part of the older Roman *mores* and *virtus* might be restored in the age in which he lived, and he may have wished, as far as in him lay, to further that restoration. But comparisons with Virgil and Horace, as represented by his Roman odes, are misleading; for there is no proof that Livy aimed deliberately, as the two poets seem to have done, at promoting the plans of Augustus. Furthermore, it is at least open to question whether Livy's admiration for the emperor was as unqualified as theirs. Had it been, would one not have expected to find a full treatment of Augustus' various reforms in the latest Books of the *History*? But, as we have already seen, what little evidence there is suggests, on the contrary, that the historian avoided these topics or treated them summarily. Hence, while Livy was an Augustan in the sense that he was a child of his age, we are hardly justified in seeing in his portraits of the good kings or in the orations of the statesmen who guided Roman destinies during the early Republic a subtle propaganda for the prince whose subject he was.

We come finally to Livy's brilliant gifts as a narrator. Some critics have sought to narrow down his achievement by arguing that his main success is attained in his descriptions of brief or isolated episodes. But Livy is no mere miniaturist; his art is as great and as compelling when he paints on a large canvas. There is a grand sweep in his sustained passages—the attack of the Gauls on Rome, Hannibal's march from Spain to Italy, Marcellus' operations culminating in the capture of Syracuse, and many others. He generally avoids the excursus; but the narrative is at times lightened or diversified by episodes which are not indeed essential to the main story but nevertheless are suggested by it. Such are the much disputed chapter on the earliest forms of Roman and Italian drama, the amusing tale how the flute players' guild won confirmation of its ancient privileges, the quarrel of the Roman matrons and the introduction of the cult of Chastity (*Pudicitia*), or tragic episodes like the death of the Capuan aristocracy or the story of Theoxena.[32] The episode of the flute players, which Livy tells in a few vivid sentences, is a good example of his simpler narrative. It is also related by Ovid and Plutarch and clearly rests on a genuine folk tradition connected with an old festival, the lesser Quinquatrus, held on June 13.[33] According to Livy, the strike took place in 311 in the middle of the Second Samnite War. Here is his account of it:

I should pass over an episode of that year, though briefly told, if it did not appear to concern religious cult. The flute players had been forbidden by the censors of the last year to hold their banquet in the temple of Jupiter, a privilege that they had enjoyed from olden times. Highly incensed, they left in a body for Tibur, so that no one was left in Rome to play before the sacrifices. The senators were filled with pious alarm and sent a deputation to Tibur to see that the Romans got these men back. The people readily promised their help. First, they summoned the players to their council house and urged them to return to Rome. When the players refused to be driven back, the Tiburtines approached them with a proposal very true to human nature. It being a feast day, they asked the players to different houses, ostensibly to furnish the music at the banquets that were being held. There they sent them to sleep by filling them up with wine, of which players as a class are extremely fond. Then, while they were still asleep, they bound them, loaded them on carts, and drove them back to Rome. The carts were left in the forum, and the players did not come to until daylight surprised them still suffering from their carouse. At this point a big crowd collected and prevailed on them to remain. They were given the privilege of parading through the city on three days every year, dressed in fancy dress, singing, and free from restraint—a custom which still persists. Those who played at the performance of sacred ritual won back the right of holding their feasts in the temple.

As an example of Livy's more elaborate manner it would be hard to select a finer passage than that which describes how the glorious news of Hasdrubal's defeat in 207 came to Rome; and, *mutatis mutandis,* it is not inappropriate to our own recent experience:

The night after the battle, Nero set out for Apulia. As his column marched more quickly than when he had come from there, he reached his permanent camp and Hannibal in five days. Since no messenger had preceded him, the crowds who met him on the march were smaller, but their rejoicing was so great that people were almost delirious with happiness. No adequate account or description can be given of the state of feeling in Rome, either that in which the city had awaited the outcome in suspense or that in which it received the report of victory. Not once in all the days since the story went round that the consul Claudius had marched out did any senator leave the senate house, and the magistrates or the people the forum, from sunrise to sunset. The married women, as they could give no active help, turned to prayers and entreaties; they wandered to all the shrines, importuning the gods with supplications and vows. While the city was in this state of anxious suspense, a vague rumor got about that two cavalrymen from Narnia had arrived at the camp which guarded the pass into Umbria, and were reporting that the enemy had been cut to pieces. At first, men had heard rather than grasped the news, as something too great and joyous for understanding or belief; and the very quickness of its reception hindered its credibility, seeing that the battle was said to have been fought only two days earlier. Next a dispatch arrived, sent from camp by L. Manlius Acidinus and reporting the arrival of the Narnian troopers. This dispatch, carried through the forum to the praetor's tribunal, brought the senate out of the senate house. The people crowded up to its doors in such disorder, as each strove to be there first, that the messenger could not come near; he was dragged this way and that by men questioning him and shouting a demand that the letter be read out on the Rostra before it was read in the senate house. At length the crowds were forced back and brought under control by magistrates, and the happy news could be passed out to minds unable to grasp it. First in the senate, then at a public meeting, the dispatch was read out. According to each man's disposition, some were full of rejoicing that knew no doubts, others were incredulous until they should have heard the staff officers or a dispatch from the consuls.

Next, word came that the staff officers were drawing near. Then in truth persons of every age ran to meet them, each one eager to be the first to absorb with eyes and ears so great a joy. A continuous column of people stretched all the way to the Mulvian Bridge. The staff officers—L. Veturius Philo, P. Licinius Varus, and Q. Caecilius Metellus—arrived at the forum ringed about by a press of men of every class, some of whom kept asking the officers themselves, others their companions, what had happened. And when a man had heard that the army of the enemy and their commanding officer had been killed, that the Roman legions were intact and the consuls safe, he straightway communicated his happiness to others. When the staff officers had made their way into the senate house with difficulty, and with far greater difficulty the crowd had been pressed back and stopped from overunning the space reserved for senators, the dispatch was read aloud in the senate. Then the officers were conducted across to the public meeting. L. Veturius, after the dispatch had been read, in person explained more clearly what had occurred, to the accompaniment of tremendous applause and finally of loud shouting from the assembled people, who could scarcely contain their delight. Then they dispersed in haste, some to the temples of the gods to give thanks, some to their homes to share such happy tidings with their wives and children. The senate, inasmuch as the consuls M. Livius and C. Claudius with their army intact had destroyed the commander and legions of the enemy, decreed a three-day thanksgiving. The praetor C. Hostilius formally proclaimed this thanksgiving before the assembly and it was observed by men and women. For the entire three days all the temples were equally crowded. The married women, attired in their most formal dress, together with their children and freed from every fear, as though the end of the war had come, gave thanks to the immortal gods. This victory also stimulated the economic life of the state; from then on, men were emboldened to carry on business as in time of peace, selling, buying, lending money, and repaying debts.[31]

Livy's lifework met with instant acclaim. It superseded earlier histories, and narratives on a large scale of Republican Rome ceased to be composed, at least in Latin. But, although it became a classic, Livy's *History* from the first probably had a very restricted circulation. Its great bulk militated against its wide dissemination as a whole, but it is likely enough that single decades were copied separately. The manuscript tradition makes this probable, nor is it wholly accidental that that tradition is best for the first and third decades. These two sections of the work held a greater attraction than any others, especially for the medieval reader. Each contained a story of unsurpassed interest, the one the growth of Rome from humble beginnings to the leadership of Italy, the other her epic struggle with a rival power in the Mediterranean, the outcome of which laid the foundation for

Imperial Rome. In both decades also Livy had found the chief secret of Rome's progress, to the point where she became a world power, in the soundness of her institutions and the purity and even austerity of manners that characterized her people. This aspect of the first and third decades also operated strongly in favor of their popularity in the medieval period, and we must surely hope that the good Abbot of Pomposa at the end of the eleventh century finally acquired what he wanted. His copy of the first decade lacked forty chapters, which "he was panting greedily to find."[35] The *History* as a whole was too long to become truly popular; hence, much-abbreviated versions, like that by Florus in the age of Hadrian, or brief summaries like the surviving epitomes, were compiled. That they contained only a small part of the substance and none of the inspiration of the original did not hinder their wide circulation.[36]

## CHAPTER VI

# TACITUS AND HIS FORERUNNERS

STUDENTS of classical literature, in their preoccupation with the surviving poets and prose writers of Greece and Rome, are sometimes apt to forget how small a proportion of ancient works in prose and verse has actually been transmitted intact. How far the disappearance of so much good, bad, and indifferent literature is the result of time and chance, and how much to the critical sense of the ancients themselves, will always be a moot point. But at least it will hardly be disputed that after the death of Augustus Roman literature was relatively poor in authors of distinction. Discerning contemporaries were not unaware of the decline that set in after the rare brilliance of the Augustan age. Quintilian composed a treatise, unhappily lost, to explain the reasons for the "corruption" of Latin prose, and Tacitus treated much the same theme in his earliest work. In form and spirit the *Dialogus* recaptures something of the freshness of the Golden age of Cicero. It has been customary to follow the lead given by these two writers and to blame the poverty of Latin literature in the first century on the existing political conditions.[1] It is the loss of political liberty which is regarded as the chief reason for the decline. This explanation is doubtless sound as far as it goes, but it does not go very far; for in other ages a great literary or artistic florescence has not always been incompatible with despotic government. In Rome it was in the long run a fatal weakness that literature and philosophy were predominantly in the hands of the ruling class; for the others there was rarely either the incentive or the opportunity for intellectual pursuits. Education, at least beyond the elementary stage, was restricted to a minority. And even had it been more widespread, ancient conditions made

---

[1] For notes to chapter vi, see pages 176–178.

the dissemination of literature among all but a small number impossible. Again, the Roman, though by no means merely imitative, nevertheless compared to the Greek was somewhat lacking in imagination and in intellectual curiosity. Pure literature may have declined in quality during the Hellenistic age, but the lively and inquiring mind of the Greek found fresh outlets for speculative activity in the field of science. Not so the Roman whose original contributions, as has often been observed, were in the more immediately practical spheres of civil engineering and law. Too little is known about the common man in the Roman imperial age to estimate the degree of his intellectual interests. The schools of rhetoric and the public declamations which Juvenal found so wearisome again attracted only a minority; and it was this minority in the first century which found far more pleasure in the chatty though often vapid collection of anecdotes drawn from Greek and Roman history and put together by Valerius Maximus than in more sober historical works. That rhetoric could and did at times exert a vicious influence on historical composition was an old complaint, and it was voiced again in the age of the Antonines. Lucian, whose own views on the writing of history were in the main borrowed from Thucydides, castigated contemporary Greek historians of the wars between Parthia and Rome, because their narratives abounded in absurdities of every kind. Lucian's portentous gravity in treating these fanciful compilers was doubtless assumed. Certainly an author who could relate that twenty-seven persons died of sheer fright when General Priscus let out his battle cry, or could describe the man-eating dragons which the Parthians trained for use in war, was an ancient Münchausen, fully conscious that he was catering for readers who wanted not sober history but an exciting yarn decked out with all the meretricious adornments of contemporary rhetorical taste. Still, Lucian preserves one story that ought to be better known than it is. He echoes Thucydides when he maintains that the historian should write not so much for the people of his own age as for posterity, and then he illustrates his point as follows: The Greek architect Sostratus, having completed the famous lighthouse at Alexandria by orders of Ptolemy II, carved his own name on a stone, covered it with cement, and then on this fresh surface inscribed the name of his royal master. After a few years Ptolemy's name disappeared as the cement wore off; then Sostratus' name became visible and remained so for future generations to behold.

Historical literature composed in the first century of the Christian era was abundant; it does not appear to have been more than mediocre in quality. Quintilian names Servilius Nonianus and Aufidius Bassus with qualified approval. The former was "more restrained than is fitting for the dignity of history"; Bassus, whose *History of the German Wars* is specifically mentioned, is "praiseworthy in all his works, but in some does not do himself full justice." Another writer who is praised more highly, though his name is withheld, was probably Fabius Rusticus. To these three, if one may accept the conjecture of a modern editor, was added Cremutius Cordus, whose *History* Quintilian only knew in expurgated form. Tacitus' judgments are more uncompromising; but, since he is by no means as free from bias as he would have us believe, they had best be treated with reserve. He is, however, consistent with his own main thesis when he observes that historical writing suffered eclipse because of the political conditions confronting authors between the accession of Tiberius and the death of Domitian. Let us hear his own words:

This *History* begins with the second consulship of Servius Galba and the first of Titus Vinius. The preceding eight hundred and twenty years from the founding of the city have been chronicled by many who wrote with equal eloquence and freedom so long as the history of the Roman people was their theme; but when Actium had been fought, and the interests of peace required that all power should be centred in one man, those great writers wrote no more, and historical truth was violated in divers ways: at first, from men's ignorance of public affairs, as though they concerned them not; afterwards, by the spirit of adulation, or of hatred towards our rulers—the hostility of some, the servility of others, shutting out all regard for posterity. But while a writer's partiality soon revolts the reader, detraction and malignity are drunk in with greedy ears: for whereas the former is open to the foul charge of sycophancy, the latter makes a false show of liberty.[3]

The prevailing fashion seems to have favored the writing of contemporary history, and those who undertook it were evidently not deterred by the difficulties which a century later disturbed the younger Pliny. In a letter to his friend Titinius Capito he explains at length that he is too busy with legal work in the courts to think of historical writing for the present. He then continues:

However, do you now reflect on this, on what period of history am I to begin? Former times, which others have described? The research in that case has been done, but comparing the various histories will be heavy work. Recent times, which no one has touched? This would cause offense to many and please few; for, in addition to the circumstance that in a very vicious age there must be far more to blame than to praise, you will be called niggardly of approval if you praise, too severe, if you censure; and that, although you have done the former lavishly, the latter with the greatest restraint.[4]

At all events, the historians of the first century are little more than names. They composed *Histories* of their own times, though some, like Cremutius Cordus and the elder Seneca, tried to bridge the present and the recent past by including accounts of the civil wars in their works. Bassus, too, in addition to his special study of Rome's wars against the German tribes, composed a general *History* from 44 B.C. to the later years, or possibly to the death, of Claudius.[5] The elder Pliny, following the example of Bassus, and doubtless also because his own interest had been aroused when in the course of his official career he stayed for a while on

the Rhine, compiled a lengthy monograph on the Roman wars
in Germany, as well as a general *History,* planned as a continuation of Bassus' and carried down to the early years of Vespasian.
If we may judge from his one surviving work, the *Natural
History,* we may believe that his historical compilations were as
full of factual information but no more attractive to read than
an encyclopedia. These two works and the *Histories* of Cluvius
Rufus and of Fabius Rusticus appear, as we shall see, among the
sources specifically named by Tacitus.

If the writers named so far are shadowy figures, the Emperor
Claudius as scholar and author is hardly more distinct. His biographer relates that, owing to his sickly youth and his inability
to follow the normal duties and avocations of a member of the
imperial family, Claudius found compensation in study and composition. Encouraged as a boy by Livy, he ended by writing
voluminously on historical and antiquarian subjects. Extensive
memoirs, a work on Carthage in eight Books, and one on the
Etruscans in twenty, and an elaborate *History of Rome* were his
most ambitious efforts. The last-named was originally planned
to begin with the assassination of Julius Caesar. When two Books
of it had been composed, Claudius abandoned his intention of
treating the civil war, as being too controversial, and made a fresh
start, beginning with the peace after Actium. We do not know
at what point he broke off, but his *History* when completed ran
to forty-one Books! While it would perhaps be unfair to say that
all these children of the emperor's brain were still-born, the fact
remains that they left next to no trace. Portions from them were
recited during Claudius' lifetime, and no doubt were admired
to his face and criticized behind his back. But the very few
extant fragments are all to be found in a single author, that om-
nivorous reader of iron digestion, Pliny the elder. It has also been
conjectured that the passage in which Tacitus, before recording
Claudius' addition of three new letters to the Latin alphabet,

traces the history of that invention, is derived from the emperor's own monograph on the subject.[9]

There is a certain irony in the fact that none of these *opera multi sudoris* have survived even in part, whilst the modest compendium of Roman history by Velleius Paterculus has for the most part been preserved. Velleius, who had served as an officer under Tiberius on the German front and later on followed an official career until he attained the praetorship, seems to have left little mark on his own or later generations; indeed, his book narrowly escaped oblivion, for our text depends on the *editio princeps* and one late manuscript, both copied from the same codex, now lost. Until recently it has as a rule been harshly judged, although De Quincey in his essay on Style praised it with enthusiasm. Admittedly this compendium is inaccurate and its manner is at times ludicrously overrhetorical; furthermore, Velleius' praise of Tiberius and Sejanus knew no limits. Yet the little book is not devoid of merit or interest. The first section, after a few introductory chapters on Greece, sketches Roman history down to 146 B.C.; but much of this part is lost, so that the extant Roman portion only begins with the Third Macedonian War. The second section opens after the final destruction of Carthage, which Velleius, following Sallust and others, regards as the beginning of a process of degeneration. "The elder Scipio," he says, "had opened the way for Roman domination, the younger Scipio opened the way for luxury. For when the fear of Carthage was past and Rome's rival for empire had been removed, the descent from virtue was not step by step, but followed a headlong course. The old discipline was abandoned, the new took its place. The state turned from watchfulness to sleep, from arms to pleasure, from active pursuit of affairs to ease."[10] Book II ends in A.D. 30. The treatment is narrowly biographical, so that much of the compendium reads like a series of short "lives" strung together rather loosely. This leads inevitably to distortion, since single individuals are given credit or made responsible for acts and developments that were the result of more complex circumstances. Velleius introduces a few digressions; for instance, a list of Roman colonies founded in Italy and a summary showing the gradual acquisition of the provinces. This demonstrates a certain breadth of view on his part, and the same quality is apparent when, in what is after all a brief survey, he still finds room for some details about the more notable personages in Roman literature. He also poses a question which, he says, he has often pondered but never stopped to think through clearly. "Who," he remarks, "can wonder enough that in every profession the most distinguished minds have concentrated on the same form of activity and been brought together within the same narrow period of time."[8] He goes on to give various examples: the short florescence of Greek tragedy and comedy in fifth-century Athens, the achievements of Greek philosophy between Socrates and Aristotle; and Roman examples also. Thus he says of Roman historical writing: "The historians too, if one adds Livy to the writers of the preceding epoch, were produced in less than eighty years, with the exception of Cato and a few obscure older authors." As to the reason for this phenomenon, he observes: "It follows that the greatest impediment to perfection in any work is man's frequent and unstable transition to other pursuits." You may call this a lame and impotent conclusion and accuse Velleius of a certain naïveté; yet the question has been asked in and about other ages and no certain answer has been forthcoming.

Perhaps the most remarkable feature of the compendium is the way in which the author links the Republic to the Imperial age. The reader is scarcely made conscious of the deep-seated revolution ushered in by Julius Caesar and completed by his great-nephew, who appears as the restorer of the old traditional form of the Republic (*prisca illa et antiqua rei publicae forma*).[9] Velleius' admiration for Augustus was great, for Tiberius it was unbounded. It is this especially which has hurt his reputation, above all with those who have accepted the Tacitean portrait of Tiberius as historically accurate. Velleius' fulsome periods become intelligible if three things are remembered: He affects a rhetorical style, but does not have it completely under his control. Then, as every reader of seventeenth- or eighteenth-century literature is aware, the praises of a patron that may now sound extravagant were once a fashion and were recognized as such by panegyrist and recipient alike. The views expressed by Dr. Johnson in his famous letter to Lord Chesterfield, whatever the motive that inspired them, were exceptional in that age. Thirdly, and above all, Velleius' long service in the army under Tiberius had aroused in him a real and deep affection and admiration for his former commander-in-chief. Furthermore, much truth underlies his hyperbolic eulogy; for there is now every reason to believe that the favorable estimate of Augustus' successor was general in Italy and the Empire, except among members of the senatorial class, whose spokesman to posterity was the embittered and satirical genius to whom we must now turn.

Cornelius Tacitus, whom it is customary to regard as Rome's greatest historian, was born not later than A.D. 58. The known facts of his life are scanty, but he fulfilled one of the necessary qualifications for a historian as laid down by Polybius; for, before turning to authorship, he acquired considerable experience of public affairs. He was probably the son of an equestrian official who at one time was procurator of Belgic Gaul. In 88 he attained the praetorship and also became a member of the priestly College of Fifteen. He himself indicates rather vaguely that he had started on his senatorial career under Vespasian and Titus. He had married the daughter of Julius Agricola, and after his father-in-law's death he was absent from Rome for several years. At last, in 97, he became consul suffectus, and thereafter, according to his friend the younger Pliny, he greatly distinguished himself as a speaker.

Through the chance recovery of an inscription from Mylasa in southwestern Asia Minor we know that he crowned his official career by holding the proconsulate of Asia in the later years of Trajan's reign (*ca.* 112?). The date of his death is unknown.[10]

The *Germania* and the *Life of Agricola* seem both to have appeared in the year after his consulship. The former is a treatise on the manners and customs of the Germanic peoples taken as a whole and concludes with a series of observations on particular tribes or tribal groups. Various theories have been put forward in modern times to explain why Tacitus composed this monograph, most of them being as fanciful as they are unconvincing. It has been interpreted as a veiled manifesto against further Roman aggression; but Trajan was certainly the last man on earth to be deterred by any tract for the times from carrying out military plans against Germanic tribes whom he regarded as a menace. Scarcely less improbable is the view that the *Germania* is a moral tract, composed to contrast the simplicity of German manners with the luxurious degeneracy of the ruling class in Rome. To argue thus is to make Tacitus into a kind of forerunner of the Christian writer Salvian, who consciously set himself to scourge the Roman society of his day and to idealize the invaders of the Empire. The proud Roman senator would hardly have appreciated the comparison or the implication. It is quite clear that there existed in the first century a keen interest in the trans-Rhenane tribes and the Roman campaigns against them, and both Aufidius Bassus and the elder Pliny had written at length on this subject. It is reasonable to suppose that Tacitus, who was already contemplating a larger historical work, wished to try his apprentice hand on some simpler subject and at the same time to popularize for educated readers the ample but possibly unreadable material brought together by these earlier investigators. Even so, one can think of short popular biographies and essays composed in our own time by facile authors who have

done no more than skim the cream off some elaborate and standard work unread except by specialists.

In the *Agricola* many of the characteristics that one associates
with Tacitus' longer works are already discernible. The emphasis
laid on the human side of his subject and on personalities was, of
course, entirely in place in what is in form a biography and in
spirit a funeral laudation. Yet Agricola does not quite come to
life, partly because the lighter touches and the little anecdotes
are missing. Slight in themselves, it is these that throw light on
the complex psychology of a man and make Plutarch's worthies
living human beings. Agricola is an outstanding instance of those
*bona exempla* which were not wholly absent even in the year
of civil war.[11] The military campaigns and topographical details
are vague or sketchy and compare unfavorably with the information supplied by Pliny.[12] But the qualities which make the
*Histories* and *Annals* inimitable as literature are distinctly fore-
shadowed in the *Agricola*. The diction, the incisive judgment,
the mordant comment on men and existing conditions, can all
be illustrated in this short biography. Cogidumnus was rewarded
for his fidelity to Rome by being given the jurisdiction over certain tribes; thus "an ancient and long-recognized custom of the
Roman people was followed, whereby even kings are included
among the instruments of servitude." Or again, after describing
Agricola's measures to promote the Romanization of Britain,
Tacitus comments: "Our style of dress was admired and the
toga became fashionable. Little by little they lapsed into those
allurements to vice, the public lounge, the bath, the eloquent
banquet. In their ignorance they called it culture, when it was
part of their enslavement." Complacency and boasting on the
part of a victorious army call forth the acid reflection: "A most
unfair aspect of war is this: everyone takes credit for success,
failure is one man's responsibility." Most familiar of all are
the bitter words put into the mouth of a British chieftain to

characterize Roman imperialism as viewed by the vanquished: "auferre, trucidare, rapere falsis nominibus imperium, atque ubi solitudinem faciunt, pacem appellant."[13] The attribution to Domitian of unworthy motives for recalling Agricola after five or six years' service foreshadows the insinuations leveled in the *Annals* against Tiberius when he relieved Germanicus of his command on the Rhine.

The *Histories* seem to have been published in the opening years of the second century; then a decade or more elapsed before the *Annals* appeared. The second Book of this work was certainly composed before the death of Trajan in 117. Whether Tacitus published his two major works in sections or only as each was completed is a matter of controversy, but no certain conclusion is possible. Together they covered the period from the accession of Tiberius to the death of Domitian, but scarcely half has survived.[14] The extant portions describe the general course of events in 69 and the revolt of Civilis in 69–70; all save two years of the principate of Tiberius; and the two decades from 47 to 66.

Tacitus' observations on the function of history are in large part traditional. Its aim is moral instruction by contrasting past and present, and guidance for the future. He remarks in one place:

It is no part of my purpose to set forth every motion that was made in the Senate, but only such as were either honourable or specially disgraceful in their character. For I deem it to be the chief function of history to rescue merit from oblivion, and to hold up before evil words and evil deeds the terror of the reprobation of posterity.

The historian may also hope to instruct his contemporaries so that they learn greater prudence in political life.

For but few have wisdom enough of their own to distinguish what is honourable from what is base, the expedient from the hurtful; most men have to learn these things from the experience of others. . . . Then again, the writer of ancient history finds few to criticize him; it concerns no one if he praise too warmly the armies of Carthage or Rome.

But there are many living now whose ancestors suffered punishment, or incurred disgrace, under Tiberius; and even if the families concerned have died out, there are those who deem an attack upon vices akin to their own to be an attack upon themselves. Even glory and virtue have their enemies; for when placed too close to their opposites they wear an aspect of rebuke.[15]

Although Tacitus contrasts the historians of a preceding age with those of his own, the teaching by example holds good in either case. Already in the *Agricola* he had remarked, with his father-in-law in mind, "even under bad rulers there can be great men." In the *Histories* he again stressed the value of historical *exempla:* "Such and suchlike stories of a former time I shall deem it not unfitting to relate whenever circumstance or place shall suggest a noble example, or afford solace for present ills."[16]

All this does not take one very far, for it does not explain the unique character of Tacitus' mind and work. It does not dispose of the antinomy, which must strike every serious student, between Tacitus the writer and Tacitus the historian. His modern critics in their search for the essential clue have reached very contrary conclusions. He has been credited with a consistent philosophy of life; he has been portrayed as under the domination throughout his literary activity of an abstract idea, the old Roman *virtus;*[17] he has been called an admirer of Republican government and institutions and, on the other hand, a champion of the Augustan principate. In the opinion of Reitzenstein, Tacitus, who began as an admirer of the principate, ended by looking back to the older Roman *res publica* as his ideal.[18] Imperialism, in the sense of a profound belief in Rome's mission to conquer and Romanize her neighbors, has been regarded as a leading, even as the dominant, principle in his thought.[19] One writer of eminence goes so far as to call Tacitus "the profoundest psychologist in history," another critic observes that "his psychology was superficial."[20] The truth seems to be that specific labels such as

Republican, Imperialist, Monarchist should not be attached to Tacitus. Apart from the danger of employing terms whose modern connotation may make them inapplicable in an ancient setting and therefore may confuse the issue, Tacitus was essentially a man of his age, and that age was in general marked by an absence of settled and clearly defined ideas in philosophy and religion. Even in politics there was both acceptance and criticism of the new order, but the critics, so far as we can tell, had no practicable alternative to suggest. The teaching of the philosophic schools was eclectic, even though the old labels persisted. There was an endless variety in religious cults and beliefs—the formal ritual of the state religion, emperor worship, Oriental cults, mystical and orgiastic, astrology, and demonology. Hence to attribute to Tacitus any consistent body of thought on life and on history involves doing violence to the evidence and reading into the historian's mind the concepts of another age.

Thirty-five years ago von Pöhlmann performed a valuable service when he analyzed Tacticus' view of life and showed, by a careful comparison of numerous passages in his writings, that it was full of contradictions. He erred, however, in applying as the yardstick wherewith to measure the historian the nineteenth-century rationalism in which he had himself become steeped.[21] Some examples will make this lack of consistency in Tacitus clearer. There is a remarkable passage in which, after describing Tiberius' interest in astrology and his friendship with its leading practitioner, Thrasyllus, Tacitus confesses: "As for myself, when I hear tales of this kind, my mind remains in doubt whether human affairs are ordered by Fate and unchangeable necessity, or proceed by chance."[22] He goes on to point out that opinion on the operation of fate in human affairs has varied, some thinkers being out-and-out determinists, others trying to find room for the freedom of the will. It is clear from the sentence quoted, and from his final remarks, that he did not reject astrology outright.

Besides, the attribution of occurrences to fate is found elsewhere in his works, with or without qualifying comment.[23] On the other hand, there are sundry allusions to Fortune. There are passages in which he is frankly contemptuous of what he calls popular superstition; yet elsewhere he seems to accept the possibility of supernatural intervention in human affairs and gives no hint of skepticism.[24] After observing that love of power leads to political unrest and even revolutions, he continues:

Legions composed of Roman citizens did not lay down their arms at Pharsalia and Philippi: much less would the armies of Otho and Vitellius have abandoned war of their own free will. The same wrath of the gods, the same human frenzy, the same criminal aims, were driving them on to strife; and that these wars were ended as it were at a single stroke, was due to the incapacity of the leaders.[25]

If it be objected that the words *deum ira* are no more than conventional phraseology, this explanation would certainly not hold good in two other passages. Tacitus sketches the career of Sejanus and then emphasizes the complete ascendancy that he gained over the emperor, "not so much through any cunning of his own—for in that quality he was himself outmatched—as from Divine wrath against the Roman Commonwealth, on which he brought disaster alike in his triumph and in his fall." Still more astonishing is Tacitus' comment, after he has described at length the conspiracy of Piso in A.D. 65 and the many deaths and executions that it brought in its train:

If I were telling of foreign wars, and of men dying for their country in ways thus like each other, I should even so be surfeited, and expect my readers to feel weariness and disgust at this long sad tale of citizens coming, however nobly, to their end; but the story of all this servile endurance, all this blood wasted wantonly at home, wears out the mind and wrings the soul with melancholy. Nor can I ask my readers to accept any other plea than this—that I cannot blame the men who perished thus ingloriously. For these things came of the wrath of the gods against Rome—a wrath that may not be passed over, as when armies are routed or cities captured, with a single mention.

And yet, a few chapters later, Tacitus, after naming a certain Cassius Asclepiodotus who suffered for standing loyally by Soranus to the end, adds: "He was now stripped of his property and banished; so unconcernedly do the gods regard examples of good and evil."[20] When we find the same writer at one time taking refuge in determinism, at another blaming the gods for human catastrophes, and at yet another enunciating a doctrine of divine noninterference in the affairs of men, we are surely justified in describing his religious ideas as unstable, if not confused.

Tacitus' political views are not marked by any special consistency either, even though they are less full of contradictions than his religious beliefs. It has been maintained that in his earliest work, the *Dialogus,* one of the speakers, Maternus, is made to voice Tacitus' own opinions, but this is a pure assumption. Tacitus was a thorough master of rhetoric and had also studied to good purpose the dialogue form as used by Cicero. Of all those who take part in the discussion Aper alone represents the "modernist" point of view, the others are agreed in stressing the superiority of Republican eloquence. Messalla, however, contrasts oldtime education with that of his own age, greatly to the advantage of the former, and points to the change in political conditions as the main reason for the decay of eloquence. The concluding speech of Maternus gathers together the various points that the previous speakers had made; but, while he too bestows the highest praise on the oratory of a bygone age, he is critical of the type of government under which that oratory attained its greatness. Thus, as it would seem, Tacitus has skillfully juxtaposed different interpretations of past and present, but there is no more reason for identifying his own notions with those of Maternus than with the opinions of Messalla. Even so in Cicero's *De oratore* it would be rash simply to equate Cicero's views with those of Crassus or of Antonius; nor is Cicero's own position, apart from his unfailing hostility to the doctrines of Epicurus, always clearly defined in the philosophical dialogues.[27]

The famous words in which Tacitus only two years after the death of Domitian hailed a new dispensation under which liberty again became possible, are no more than a natural expression of relief at the cessation of a harsh despotism; for, as the context shows, Tacitus is by no means sure how quickly men will recover from the political demoralization in which they had been sunk for fifteen years.[28] And what of the principate which had long been irreconcilable with liberty? Doubtless the Augustan principate was a very different thing from the autocracy of a Domitian; but, though Tacitus in A.D. 98 may have looked back to it as a satisfactory and on the whole equitable regime, did he continue so to regard it when he had studied it more closely? The opening chapters of the *Annals* suggest the direct contrary. The summary description of Octavian's rise to power is certainly not flattering; and there is an undercurrent of bitterness also in what is said about Augustus' dynastic plans. A little later, the historian, borrowing the technique, as it were, of the rhetorical schools with their *suasoriae* and *controversiae*,[29] affects to reproduce the various comments made after Augustus' death on the deceased princeps and his rule. First we are given some fifteen lines of modified approval of Augustus for carrying through the stabilization and assuring the security of Italy and the Empire after the civil wars; but then there follows a passage more than twice as long and filled with detraction. Octavian before Actium is represented as an unscrupulous adventurer who stopped at nothing to sweep all rivals from his path. Next come animadversions on Augustus' private affairs and family, on the introduction of the imperial cult, and on his policy in finally adopting Tiberius as his successor. Surely, if Tacitus had admired Augustus and his work of reconstruction, this was an odd way in which to show it. Actually, it is not unfair to say that he nowhere mani-

fests the slightest appreciation or understanding of Augustus'
achievement. It is true that in another passage, after a brief review of Roman history especially since the Gracchi, he continues:
"At last in his sixth consulship Caesar Augustus, now his power
was secure, canceled the acts that he had decreed during the triumvirate and imposed a constitution under which we should
enjoy peace and a prince." But what are his next words? "From
then on our bonds were stricter, watchmen were set over us, and
under the Lex Papia Poppaea were attracted by rewards, so that
if a man failed to earn the profits of parenthood, the people as a
common parent might own the vacant property."[30] It is clear
from the reference to the Lex Papia Poppaea of A.D. 9 that Tacitus still has the principate of Augustus in mind, although he then
passes on to the activity of the informers under Tiberius. There
is significance, moreover, in the order of the words, "deditque
iura quis pace et principe uteremur." Tacitus has deliberately
put *principe* after *pace* to show his irony: "A constitution under
which we should enjoy peace—and a prince," that is to say, peace
but at the cost of having a princeps.[31]

One can detect a certain change in Tacitus' attitude to the
order of which he was himself so distinguished a member. In
the *Histories* there is an unmistakable streak of sympathy for the
senatorial opposition headed by Helvidius Priscus. In the *Annals*
there is unrelieved contempt for the senate, which is represented
as sinking lower and lower in its process of degradation from the
time of Tiberius to that of Nero. If a Thrasea arouses his just
admiration, it is as a man, not as a senator. There is one feature
of Roman government in the first century which Tacitus saw
very clearly and, with sound historical insight, kept steadily before the eyes of his readers. He has often been described as an
unmilitary historian, and this is true, as it is of most other ancient
historians, in the sense that his accounts of battles and campaigns
are often vague and rhetorical. But he did perceive the transcend-

ent importance of the military in the sphere of politics, in determining the fate of Rome and the Empire. Again and again it is the *soldatesca* which appears in his pages as the real arbiter of Roman fortunes.

In conclusion, we must refer briefly to the problem of Tacitus' sources. Attempts have been made to prove that he followed one main source in the *Histories* and one in the *Annals,* but, as we have noted of Livy, such a method is arbitrary and at variance with such evidence as exists. Thus, when Tacitus refers to "writers" or "authors" in the plural, we should take him at his word. Again, the historian whom he is supposed to have followed in preference to any other when composing the earlier Books of the *Annals* is Aufidius Bassus; yet the fact remains that Bassus is never mentioned in the historical works at all! He and his contemporary, Servilius Nonianus, are contrasted in the *Dialogus* with Varro and Sisenna in the matter of style or literary qualities (*eloquentia*). It is more than likely that Tacitus did turn to Bassus, just as he consulted Cluvius, Fabius Rusticus, and the elder Pliny in the later parts of the *Annals;* for these authors are mentioned by name.[32] Nor can it be said that any agreement has been reached by scholars through a comparison of the *Histories* with Suetonius' *Lives* of Galba, Otho, and Vitellius, with Plutarch, and with the fragments and abbreviated version of Cassius Dio. One reason for our uncertainty is that in Tacitus, as often in Livy, authorities are only invoked by name when a controversial matter is at issue. It is also doubtful what interpretation should be placed on two passages in which there is an allusion to the *Memoirs* of the younger Agrippina and to the *Memoirs* of Corbulo.[33] In the first passage the phraseology does not seem to imply a consistent use of this doubtless sensational piece of writing; in the second there is nothing to prove that Tacitus had studied Corbulo's book for himself, although, in view of his admiration for the man, he very probably had. But, since Pliny the elder names this source five times, the possibility remains that Tacitus' acquaintance with it was at second hand. In a single passage he quotes from the official record of proceedings in the senate.[34] Seeing that so much of the narrative in the *Annals* is taken up with senatorial debates and with trials before that body sitting in its judicial capacity, it has been argued by those who have Tacitus' reputation as a historian at heart that he made constant and direct use of the *acta senatus*. But they forget that a methodical study of original documents was not customary with ancient historians. Actually, the manner in which Tacitus records senatorial meetings, and especially the trials conducted before that body, makes it improbable that he habitually studied the *acta*. At all events, there is still no agreement on this point among scholars.[35]

In short, the problem of Tacitus' sources of information and their use by him is likely to remain insoluble. This circumstance, however, is relatively unimportant, for one thing is certain: Tacitus' manner of presenting his materials was peculiarly his own and his whole approach to the history of the first century was highly individualistic.

His method of indicating his sources in general terms follows a familiar pattern. Appeals to "authorities" are fairly frequent; here and there he presents oral information derived from persons contemporary with the events narrated.[36] He is on his guard against unsupported rumors and idle gossip, and even justifies himself for repeating them. After relating at some length one story long current, he gives a whole chapter to refuting it and ends with this general apology:

My reason for repeating and refuting this tale is by means of an outstanding example to rebut false rumours and to beseech those into whose hands my book shall fall, not eagerly to accept widespread and unbelievable stories and give them the preference over truth not corrupted by the marvellous.

After the astonishing description of Claudius' death, which displays his narrative powers at their best, he admits the strangeness of the tale and adds the brief comment: "But this is not a story made up for marvel's sake. I shall record only what was heard and written down by my elders."[37] This may mean conversation with a survivor from those times, but it may also refer to a type of fugitive literature the existence of which is vouched for by the younger Pliny. He states that one C. Fannius composed a book describing the "last moments" of persons put to death or banished by Nero; he also attributes a similar compilation, but without giving any particulars, to his friend and correspondent, Capito.[38] It is not improbable that some such collections were consulted and utilized by Tacitus.[39]

The source problem in Tacitus, then, is of quite secondary interest. To form a just appraisal of his merits and faults as a historian we must first consider whether his interpretations are consistent with the facts that he records. Then, in the second place, we must test the truth of his historical presentation in the light of our present knowledge of the Roman Empire in the first century. To this task we must address ourselves in the next chapter.

## CHAPTER VII

# TACITUS, THE HISTORIAN

AT THE BEGINNING of the *Annals,* Tacitus informs his readers that he is about a write the history of Tiberius and his successors "unmoved, as I have no reason to be moved, by either hatred or partiality." If this assurance is seriously meant, and not merely a conventional tribute to the principle that a historian should be free from bias, it surely gives expression to one of the most amazing examples of self-deception in all literature.[1] It is the measure of his literary genius that he has imposed his own estimate of his work on generations of readers; for even today it is not unusual to find his portrait of Tiberius or Claudius accepted, at worst without question, at best with only slight modifications. In the preceding chapter an attempt was made to show by reference to his own writings how far from consistency his general outlook was. We must now pass on to consider his credibility as an authority on the times of which he writes; and in so doing we must, as far as possible, divorce the man of letters from the historian.

His art is not and never has been in question. At its best his skill as a narrator is unsurpassed in Latin literature. This is obvious not merely in those famous scenes in which his powers of dramatic presentation are given the fullest scope—the fall of Messalina, the last hours of Claudius and of Britannicus, the murder of the younger Agrippina, the Pisonian conspiracy and the great fire at Rome,—but throughout the *Annals* and the *Histories*. His dexterous avoidance of monotony is astonishing. The principate of Tiberius opened with serious mutinies among the legions stationed on the Rhine and in Pannonia. There was a considerable similarity between the two events, and in the hands

---

[1] For notes to chapter vii, see pages 178–179.

of a lesser writer their description would certainly have led to marked resemblances if not actual repetition. Such episodes, like battle scenes, riots, and so forth, might easily, as we have already noted, become stereotyped, in fact a rhetorical exercise. In Tacitus the structural building up of the two passages, whereby a certain dramatic climax is reached and the main action is made to center on Germanicus or Drusus, shows a certain likeness. But the art of the narrator, especially in avoiding similar phraseology, is such that the reader experiences no feeling of monotony. Precisely the same is true in other parts of Tacitus. The earlier Books of the *Annals* are filled with senate meetings, or trials before that body under the law of *maiestas*. The reader may grow weary of the repeated prosecutions of leading men, or the rather empty deliberations of the Fathers, but at least he will encounter constant variety in the presentation of events basically alike. Two of the most harassing episodes related in the *Histories* are the sack of Cremona and the sack of Rome after a fight between the Vitellians and the soldiers of Antonius Primus.[2] The attendant circumstances—rape, torture, or murder of innocent persons, looting, bestiality of every kind—are the same, but again Tacitus' mastery of language is such that there is no trace of that generic likeness which even Livy was not always able to avoid. Or again, to take a simpler example, one can contrast the two descriptions that Tacitus introduces of what was no rare occurrence in Rome and the vicinity—a flooding of the Tiber attended by loss of life, destruction of property, and temporary homelessness. Such an inundation took place in A.D. 69, and he sketches the disaster in a few vivid words:

But the greatest alarm of all—one in which fears for the future were joined with present disaster—was caused by a sudden inundation of the Tiber. Coming down in immense volume, its waters carried away the Sublician Bridge; and being thrown back by the obstructing mass, flooded not only the level and low-lying parts of the city but those also which were thought to be safe from such calamities. Many persons were swept away in the streets; many more were cut off in their shops and sleeping-chambers; lack of food and earnings brought about a famine among the common people. The foundations of tenements were sapped by the standing water, and gave way when it subsided. And as soon as men's minds had been relieved from these fears, and Otho was preparing to set forth, the fact that his way to the war through the Campus Martius and by the Flaminian Way was blocked, instead of being referred to chance or to its natural causes, was interpreted as a portent, ominous of impending calamity.[3]

A similar catastrophe had occurred in A.D. 15. Tacitus records it more briefly, but adds a discussion about possible measures for the future control of the river, besides using the occasion to bring in one of his many sneers at the emperor:

In the same year the Tiber, swollen by continuous rains, flooded the lower parts of the city, and much destruction of life and property followed on the subsidence of the waters. Asinius Gallus proposed that the Sibylline books should be consulted; but this Tiberius would not permit, loving mystery in all things, divine as well as human. It was remitted to Ateius Capito and Lucius Arruntius to devise a plan for keeping the river within its banks.

These two subsequently raised the question of appropriate measures, which would have affected a good many municipalities to the north of Rome, and there was discussion in the senate, and deputations from the towns were heard. Tacitus ends his account sardonically: "Whatever the reason that prevailed—whether it was the remonstrance of the towns, or the difficulty of the work, or the appeal to religious sentiment—Piso's motion in favour of leaving things as they were carried the day."[4] How strangely modern it all sounds!

Most remarkable of all for their descriptive power are the last hours and deaths of a long gallery of persons. The pages of Tacitus are crowded with such scenes, portraying the end of Tiberius, Claudius, Messalina and Agrippina, Britannicus, the three short-lived emperors of A.D. 69, to say nothing of the victims of the Tiberian and Neronian "terror" as imagined by the historian. Whatever the source from which the facts were derived,[5] there is no repetition in treatment, each scene has individual characteristics. To show this, it is not necessary to do more than to set side by side the deaths of Galba and of Vitellius, which in their grim brutality were strikingly similar:

As soon as this armed force appeared upon the scene, the standard-bearer of the cohort in attendance upon Galba (they say his name was Atilius Vergilio) tore off the Emperor's effigy, and dashed it to the ground. At this signal all the soldiers declared openly for Otho; the populace fled; the Forum was left deserted; swords were drawn against all who hesitated. Galba's panic-stricken bearers got as far as the Curtian pool, where he was thrown from his chair and rolled upon the ground.

His last words were variously reported, as each man's admiration or hatred prompted. Some say that he imploringly asked, *What harm had he done? Might he not have a few days to pay the donative?* The more common account is that he presented his throat to his murderers, bidding them *be quick and strike, if so they thought best for the Commonwealth.* But the murderers cared not what he said; nor is it known for certain who struck the fatal blow. Some say it was a veteran called Terentius; others one Laecanius; but the generally received account is that a soldier of the 15th Legion, Camurius by name, cut his throat right through with one stroke of his sword. Others inflicted ghastly wounds on his arms and legs (his breast being protected by the cuirass), or with brutal ferocity struck at his now headless body.[6]

The assassination of Vitellius is as starkly realistic, yet how different in detail!

After the capture of the city, Vitellius was carried in a chair through the back part of the Palace to his wife's house on the Aventine, intending, if he could conceal himself during the day, to take refuge with the cohorts of his brother at Terracina. Then with his usual inconstancy of purpose, and with the natural tendency of a man who fears

everything to be most disquieted by what he sees before him, he returned to the desolate and deserted Palace, where even the lowest of
the menials had either slunk away or shrank from meeting him. He
was terrified by the solitude and the silence; he tried closed doors and
shuddered at the emptiness. Wearied at last with his wretched wan-
dering, he concealed himself in a mean hiding-place, whence he was
dragged forth by the Tribune of a cohort, Julius Placidus. Then with
his hands bound behind his back, and his clothes torn, he was led
along, a hideous spectacle, amid the curses of many and the tears of
none, all pity quenched by the unseemly manner of his end. One of
the German soldiers in his path, either in anger, or to save him from
further outrage, aimed a blow at him—or possibly at the Tribune:
the man cut off the Tribune's ear and was immediately dispatched.

Vitellius was compelled by sword-points to hold up his head and
offer it to insult; then to look at his statues as they fell, and to gaze
again and again at the Rostra, and the spot where Galba had been mur-
dered. He was finally thrust out on the Gemonian Stairs, where the
body of Flavius Sabinus had lain.

One saying alone of a not ignoble kind was he heard to utter in
answer to the insults of the Tribune: *Yet I was once your Emperor!*
He then fell under a multitude of blows; the men reviled him when
slain with the same baseness with which they had fawned on him
when alive.'

These two passages fully demonstrate Tacitus' descriptive powers. They are also instructive because they illustrate his practice
of recording variations in the details of presumably contemporary accounts; and, lastly, they show the uncompromising,
indeed brutal, realism of his method. In this respect he differs
greatly from Livy, who inclines to leave the crasser details of
war and violent death undescribed. Thus it happens that we have
both his and Polybius' account of the horrors witnessed by Philip
V at Abydos. Livy is very restrained, but Polybius particularizes
the various methods by which women and children were killed.'
Whatever the reason for Livy's reserve, it still falls short of the
grim but tremendously impressive understatement that we find
constantly in the pages of Thucydides, as, for example, in the

simple sentences that conclude his account of the Athenian disaster in Sicily.

Tacitus gave variety to his works by introducing speeches into
his narrative from time to time. It was the customary method of
indicating, especially at critical moments, the ideas and inten-
tions of important personages as handed down in the sources
or imagined by the writer. Tacitus' method underwent some
change as he grew older. The speeches of Agricola and the British chief Calgacus are relatively long, and are good examples
of skillful rhetoric, hardly more. In the *Histories* they are notice-
ably shorter, there is more effort at individual characterization
and more contrast between the speakers. We see this clearly in
the orations assigned to Galba, to his nominee for the principate,
Piso, and to his rival, Otho. The address of Otho to the Praetorian
Guard is a good example of a rabble-rousing speech. The importance of Mucianus, the "king-maker," in assuring the success of
Vespasian against his rivals is brought out by the same device,
and the address of Cerialis to two Gaulish tribes is the most sympathetic presentation in all Tacitus of Rome's civilizing mission.[9]
The discourses, both in direct and indirect speech, introduced into
the *Annals* are for the most part brief; strongly didactic in tone,
they also exhibit Tacitus' power of psychological analysis at their
highest. We shall have occasion to note, however, that they are
not always free from personal bias. A special interest attaches to
the oration delivered by Claudius in A.D. 48 in favor of granting
a petition presented by the Gauls for their admission to public
office, for the greater part of the original address, inscribed on
a bronze tablet found at Lyons, is still extant.[10] A comparison
of this text with the oration composed by Tacitus is a valuable
illustration of his method. He reproduces accurately the substance of Claudius' remarks, but he has shortened them substantially. The style is his own but with some indication of
Claudius' pedantic manner. The emperor had indulged himself

in a historical disquisition, much of the thought being directly indebted to Canuleius' speech in the fourth Book of Livy's *History*. Tacitus has cut most of this borrowed material away. He has also made some changes in the order of Claudius' observations and even added some that are not in the original. It is noticeable that this composition is free from the traits which Tacitus attributes to the emperor in several other speeches, where Claudius appears as something of a braggart and given to platitudes.

To proceed from Tacitus the great writer to Tacitus the historian is to pass from concord to controversy. Even his severest critics concede the general accuracy of the facts that he records. This can be proved, not by the unsatisfactory method of comparing his narrative with that of his inferiors, Suetonius and Dio, but by checking many of his details with evidence derived from inscriptions, coins, and other archaeological material. The many comparisons by which he is thus vindicated are sufficient to establish his zeal for truthful presentation without cavil, whereas those by which he can be proved wrong are few and usually of trifling significance. And it is certainly rare to find the other literary authorities for the period superior to him, as one of them seems to be in the following example. His account of a mutiny of Praetorians in the time of Otho has with reason been criticized. The narrative is sketchy and not readily intelligible, because the underlying reasons for the riot are not made clear. Some information provided by Suetonius, though itself slight, supplies a key to the proper understanding of the episode.[11] But, on the other hand, it is futile to test Tacitus' accuracy by a meticulous comparison of his account with that of Dio of a single occurrence like the mutiny on the Rhine in A.D. 14. Even if it could be shown conclusively that here Dio is more reliable, what does a single example prove? In reality, the differences between him and Tacitus in reporting the mutiny hinge mainly on the motives and character of Germanicus. In this respect, as distinct from the statement of facts, Tacitus must be used with caution; but so, though for other reasons, must Dio.[12]

As in other Roman historians, so in Tacitus, the topographical information and the data provided about important campaigns are insufficient. There were several good reasons for this: It is probable that detailed and accurate accounts of military operations would have appealed little to the literary public in Rome; nor would they have been suitable for oral delivery.[13] Tacitus himself, moreover, with his mind fixed on persons and the clash of personalities, seems to have had only a lukewarm interest in military history for its own sake. If there was one province and one series of operations about which he could have obtained trustworthy and full information, it was Britain and the Roman conquest of that island. Yet the exact route of Suetonius Paulinus' march from Anglesey to Colchester and London, or the site of Agricola's last great victory over the Caledonian tribes, are still matters for dispute. Similarly with the campaigns in Germany or in the Near East: their general course is usually, though not invariably, intelligible, but Tacitus' real preoccupation all the while is with Germanicus and Corbulo, two of his military heroes who are put forward in his dramatic epic as foils to the villains: in the one instance, Tiberius, in the other, Nero. One is a little reminded of Sallust's juxtaposition of Sertorius and Pompey in the *Histories*. Tacitus may have derived his estimate of Germanicus' character and achievements from his source and from popular belief. But one cannot acquit him of lack of critical acumen when he helped to perpetuate a legend and represented a conceited young man of mediocre abilities, and even not free from treasonable thoughts, into a great captain and shining hero of romance. Corbulo, of course, was in a different class. He had great experience both as a general and as an administrator. Whether he quite measured up to Lucullus or even Pompey, both of whom had campaigned in the same difficult terrain as he, is another question. And on two occasions his personal integrity and motives are not entirely above suspicion: when he entered into an agreement with Vologeses of Parthia that was later repudiated by the Roman government, and when he failed to give full support at a crucial moment to the Roman commander in Armenia. Tacitus does not wholly exonerate his hero, but leaves the issue in doubt; but his account of Paetus' operations in Armenia are scarcely intelligible without the additional information supplied by Dio. This raises the suspicion that he may be unfair to Paetus in order to enhance the glory of Corbulo.

One of the main criticisms that has often been leveled against the *Annals,* and indeed against Tacitus' whole historical outlook, is narrowness. The Roman Empire at large, its peoples and resources, and even its general administration, are almost wholly neglected. Tacitus' attention, save for occasional campaigns or other events involving the military forces of the Empire, is focused on the emperors, on the court and its intrigues, and on the governing class to which the historian himself belonged. His aristocratic feeling is very strong and he reprobates loss of caste. Livilla is censured not merely for her loose morals but for demeaning herself when she consorted with Sejanus. In recording the suicide of a senator he disapproves not so much the act itself as the method adopted. In the account of Curtius Rufus' origin the impartial reader will find that the good sense of Tiberius contrasts with the snobbery of the historian.[14] Furneaux, whose work as a commentator on Tacitus was outstanding, once magisterially asserted: "The designation of his [i.e., Tacitus'] work by St. Jerome, as 'Lives of the Caesars,' needs but to be mentioned, to show its entire inadequacy."[15] I venture to suggest that the Christian Father showed more insight than the Oxford don. Take away everything in the *Annals* not directly or indirectly connected with the emperors, and what is left? The plaint of some more recent writers that Tacitus says little or nothing about the economic resources and life of the Empire can be ignored, since it implies a judgment of Tacitus which is completely anachronistic. Where Tacitus is really vulnerable to criticism is in this: he professes to portray the character of Tiberius and Claudius and Nero, but his picture lacks essential traits, till it comes perilously near caricature. He gives a chapter to Tiberius' administration down to A.D. 23, showing that it was just and efficient.[16] But from this point on—that is to say, from the rise of Sejanus and the death of the younger Drusus—everything, according to his interpretation, was changed. His account of the first six years of Claudius' reign is lost, so we cannot tell whether they were represented as a period of relatively good government, just as the beginning of Tiberius' principate and the *quinquennium Neronis* were pictured as short eras of beneficent rule leading up to a prolonged reign of terror. The surviving narrative of Claudius' principate, from A.D. 47 to 54, is one of unrelieved gloom. Claudius, weak, eccentric almost to the point of imbecility, cruel, debauched, is little more than a pawn in the ruthless game for power played by Messalina and Agrippina and their respective allies among the influential freedmen of the emperor. There is no parallel in all history to these two pitiless and conscienceless representatives of their sex in bitter opposition, unless it be Fredegund and Brunhild in the lurid pages of Gregory of Tours. The reign of Nero is the final phase in the epic or tragedy—either term seems applicable—that Tacitus has composed on the fortunes and decline of the Julio-Claudian house. If Nero's name has become synonymous with unrestrained vice and cruelty, it is primarily thanks to Tacitus' *Annals*.

With all their brilliance these imperial portraits are distorted. The mind of Tacitus is completely enthralled by the personal characters and private lives of these emperors; their public acts and policy as rulers of a vast empire are kept in the background or ignored. Yet his candor has often and rightly been singled out for praise; for scattered through the pages of the *Annals* many facts have been set down which are irreconcilable with his imputations, and which help to controvert his interpretation of the emperors' characters. This is especially noticeable in his treatment of Tiberius. As we have seen, the general excellence of Tiberius' government down to A.D. 23 is admitted, albeit not too graciously. The fourteen years that followed are depicted as a despotism and reign of terror that grew progressively worse. Actions of Tiberius which might be recorded in his favor are interpreted in the worst light or mentioned briefly without comment. The letter addressed by the emperor to the senate about Cotta Messalinus, which was merely pathetic, is for Tacitus the outburst of a guilty conscience.[17] In A.D. 33 a grave financial crisis developed. Tacitus relates some of the measures taken to cope with it and the emperor's personal liberality; but his only comment is: "Thus was credit restored," and there is not one word of appreciation for the good sense and *liberalitas* of Tiberius. Even in his account of Tiberius' earlier years as princeps Tacitus hits below the belt. He refers to a gladiatorial exhibition at which Drusus presided, and draws attention to that prince's pleasure in bloodshed. Then he continues:

The emperor himself did not appear; for which various reasons were given. Some said that he disliked a crowd; others that he was naturally morose, and shrank from a comparison between himself and Augustus, who had graciously attended such spectacles. Another explanation was suggested which I cannot bring myself to believe; that he purposely afforded to his son an opportunity of displaying his savage temper, and thus rousing the feeling of the people against him.[18]

The historian, who elsewhere warns against idle rumors, here repeats a peculiarly malicious one himself, even though he professes to disbelieve it! The speeches and letters of Tiberius in the pages of Tacitus often show the emperor in a favorable light.[19] Though composed by the historian, they were doubtless based on reliable information. Sometimes they appear without comment, but often Tacitus cannot refrain from observations of his own, like, "popular sentiments like these were all the more acceptable that they were seldom heard from Tiberius." The emperor in a speech of great dignity addressed to the senate firmly declined divine honors for himself. Tacitus comments thus:

To this attitude he held fast thereafter, repudiating, even in conversation, any such worship of himself. Some put this down to modesty; some to want of self-confidence; others called it poverty of spirit. *The noblest of mankind,* these said, *had ever the loftiest hopes; it was thus that Hercules and Liber among the Greeks, Quirinus among ourselves, had been ranked among the Gods. Augustus had done better in not putting the hope away. All else Princes had ready to their hand; but there was one end which they should pursue unfalteringly: to leave a fair name behind them. For to despise Fame is to despise Virtue.*[20]

And then there is the final summing-up after Tiberius' death; though often quoted, it deserves to be set down once more:

His character passed through like changes to his fortunes. Admirable in conduct, and in high esteem, while in a private station, or filling commands under Augustus; dark, and artful in affecting virtue, so long as Germanicus and Drusus lived, he presented the same mixture of good and evil until his mother died. Then came a period of fiendish cruelty, but masked libertinism, during the days when he loved and feared Sejanus: until at last, freed from all fears, lost to all shame, he broke out in wickedness and wantonness alike, and showed himself in no character but his own.[21]

*Sine ira et studio?* Rather, a brilliant but remorseless satire!

There is now no doubt that the Tacitean picture of the years from A.D. 23 to 37 is radically false in many particulars. There is adequate proof that good government of the Empire at large went on as before; that Tiberius continued to the last to attend to his imperial duties conscientiously, and even that the supposed reign of terror in his declining years never took place. The unspeakable orgies on Capri have been discredited long since.[22] Even more important is the indubitable fact that Tiberius' work in carrying on and extending the civilizing mission of Augustus in Italy and the Empire earned the gratitude of the people. Hostility to him seems to have been all but confined to the senatorial class. It was amongst them or those influenced by them that Tacitus found the legend of Tiberius the Tyrant. Furthermore, Tacitus, quite apart from the one-sided and tainted sources which may have helped to form his interpretation, had lived through the despotism of Domitian. He tended to assume that conditions under the last of the Flavian emperors were the same as, or at least little different from, conditions in the age of Tiberius. Yet nothing could be more unlikely. It is conceivable that many of the senatorial class after the reign of Nero and the civil war of 69–70 were a fawning and craven crew; but to attribute a similar servility and lack of spirit to men who had grown up during the Augustan age is simply to imagine the unbelievable.

In the Books that deal with Tiberius, Tacitus, as we have seen, is constantly at pains to put the very worst construction on the emperor's words and deeds. In his account of Claudius and of Nero such comments are left aside, presumably because the historian regarded the facts that he put down as sufficiently damning by themselves. But what are the facts ascertainable about Claudius, the ruler who "was incapable of living single and was made to be ruled by his wives"?[23] He regarded Augustus with admiration, but displayed independence of judgment, so that he departed widely from the policy of that emperor. His policy in the East was more aggressive, and he undertook the conquest of Britain. While he suppressed delation and did all he could to restore the outward dignity of the senate after the extravagance of Gaius, being indeed at pains to revive the Augustan fiction of a partnership between that body and the princeps, the real significance of his principate lies in the greatly increased cen-

tralization of the government in many spheres. It was the emperor who was in control, ably assisted by his personal secretariat
of accomplished and hardworking freedmen. The prominence
of these imperial secretaries and the power that they wielded, as
long as they were sure of the emperor's good-will, were bitterly
resented by the upper class of citizens. Claudius' principate, moreover, was an age of many and often drastic changes. Many new
municipalities and especially military colonies were founded at
that time; new territory was acquired by Rome, not merely by
the conquest of southern England, but by the annexation of
Thrace. Rome's control over Mauretania was strengthened, and
in general a firm policy was pursued toward the neighbors on
her vast frontiers. Claudius' rescript to the people of Alexandria,
of which the authentic version has been recovered from a papyrus, is a statesmanlike document; unfortunately we do not know
how Tacitus interpreted this action of Claudius', since it occurred
near the beginning of his reign.[24] There were also administrative
changes of a significant kind. Some of these are recorded by Tacitus, but without appreciation of their value or importance. One
of them, the giving of increased judicial authority to provincial
procurators, was only introduced in A.D. 53. The historian cannot
have been in doubt about its importance. It has elicited from him
a historical disquisition which is so full of inaccuracies that even
so devoted an admirer as Ramsay is constrained to remark: "The
whole chapter is an outburst of senatorial indignation against the
rise of those new classes whose services had become essential for
the conduct of public business."[25]

Nero's private life may have been detestable, but in many
respects even during his principate the problems of empire continued to be handled with firmness and sagacity; nor do the
provinces, even with increased taxation, appear to have suffered
a serious decline of prosperity. Where Nero failed—and here
his personal conduct with its pseudo-Hellenism and other un-

Roman traits weighed heavily in the balance—was in his hold over the military forces of the Empire.

Tacitus' skill as a psychologist which has so often been extolled had definite limitations. Unquestionably he had a sharp eye for human failings and could pillory them with a few incisive words. "Benefactions are welcome, so long as it seems possible to repay them; when they go far beyond that limit, hatred takes the place of gratitude."[26] "Even glory and virtue have their enemies; for when placed too close to their opposites they wear an aspect of rebuke."[27] And what could be more penetrating than the remarks assigned to Paetus Thrasea?

But now we pay court to foreigners, and flatter them: one man, of his own good pleasure, may secure a vote of thanks; another may as readily bring about an accusation. And let them so resolve; let provincials retain the right of thus exhibiting their power: only let panegyrics that are false, and have been extorted by entreaty, be put down as sternly as cruelty and malicious accusation. For in general, more sins are committed from the desire to please than from a wish to injure; nay, some virtues themselves are hated: the strictness that never relaxes, the strength of soul that never yields to favour.[28]

Many of Tacitus' sketches of persons are faultless miniature portraits; but, though the choice is wide, a single instance must here suffice, the famous characterization of Petronius Arbiter, borne out, as it is, by his own work:

He passed his days in slumber, his nights in business and enjoyment. As others achieve fame by energy, so did Petronius by indolence; yet he was not looked upon as a glutton, or as a spendthrift, like other men who run through their means, but as a man who made a science of pleasure. The air of unconventionality and self-abandonment which distinguished everything that he said or did was relished all the more for wearing an appearance of simplicity. And yet as Proconsul of Africa, and afterwards as Consul, he proved himself a man of vigour, and one capable of affairs. After that, resuming a life of vice, or what affected to be vice, he was admitted into the circle of Nero's most intimate friends, and became his authority on matters of taste: Nero not thinking that anything had attained to the supreme point of charm or luxury unless it had been recommended to him by Petronius.[29]

This is a perfect little etching in which even the most carping critic could find no flaw. In these pen portraits Tacitus maintains a very high level, and exceptions are rare. One such is the comparison between Vespasian and Mucianus. The introduction of the conventional vices of *avaritia* and *luxuria,* and the trivial conclusion, hardly rise above what any senior student might have composed for his teacher of rhetoric.[30] One would not notice the passage at all were it not that the fanatical admirers of Tacitus can find it admirable.

Tacitus' outstanding weakness as a psychologist, however, is demonstrated in his portraits of the emperors. Professor Rand, whose recent death has been a grievous loss to classical and medieval studies, in his last book observed: "Tacitus, I should say, is interested primarily in the psychology of popular judgments, in the ability of a human mind, or group of minds, to twist facts into agreement with one's preconceptions."[31] This is true enough, but Mr. Rand failed to add that Tacitus himself is the best example of one who thus twists his facts. Marsh came much nearer to expressing the whole truth when he observed of Tacitus that "he conceived of character as a wholly static and immutable thing."[32] Thus, in order to explain the change which he asserts came over Tiberius in his later years Tacitus is obliged to assume that the emperor was vicious from the first but successfully dissimulated his real character to old age. Had we those Books of the *Annals* which described the opening years of Claudius' principate, we should probably find that, analogously, the historian explained the emperor's character in terms of his physical disabilities and the life of semiseclusion forced on him till he was nearing middle age. That Claudius should in large measure have overcome these weaknesses and risen to the occasion when great responsibility at last was laid on him was a development which we are justified on the evidence in assuming; but it was one, if we may judge by the extant portions of Tacitus, which would not have fitted in with his prejudices and preconceptions.

Thus our final conclusion must be that Tacitus' unique qualities as a writer should not blind us to his grave shortcomings, even by ancient standards, as a historical authority. It is not that Tacitus is merely a supreme master of words. Even where he is most rhetorical his control over his medium of expression is complete. His startling phrases and unforgettable epigrams are not dragged in just to shock or amuse the reader; they fit completely into their context and are the expression of his natural habit of thought. His chief weakness is just this: that the satirist runs away time and again with the historian. A close comparison of him with Livy is difficult and perhaps unprofitable, since the parts of Livy's *History* which for a full and fair appraisal we should need to set side by side with Tacitus have not survived. Even so, the common judgment on the two men should be reversed. For breadth of view, for his general conception of what historical writing should be, and the manner in which he gave practical expression to it, perhaps also for a more deeply rooted *humanitas,* the first place among Roman historians belongs to Livy.

The well-known prediction of the younger Pliny that the works of his friend were certain of immortality had to wait for its fulfillment until the sixteenth century. Tacitus' fame, unlike that of Livy or Edward Gibbon, was not assured overnight. No doubt in the intimate circle of his friends the *Histories* and *Annals* were justly hailed as masterpieces, but allusions to him in the later Imperial age are curiously scanty and not always trustworthy. The story that the Emperor Tacitus proudly claimed the historian as his ancestor is very suspect.[33] There is no hint anywhere of attempts to abbreviate his longer works, as was done several times with Livy's. Public taste responded more readily to purely biographical compilations, Suetonius especially, and later on the lost Marius Maximus, and finally even the *Augustan History*. In the Middle Ages, Tacitus was not quite so completely forgotten as has sometimes been affirmed. A fair number of scattered references can be assembled, which suffice to show that in the Carolingian age and afterward one or other of his works was occasionally read.[34] Yet manuscripts must have been very few. But for the survival of the two Medicean codices, containing respectively *Annals* I to VI and *Annals* XI to XVI together with the early Books of the *Histories,* these works would have disappeared entirely. In the fourteenth century, interest in Tacitus began to revive; it received an immense stimulus during the next hundred years, when the two manuscripts just mentioned and a third containing the minor works were rediscovered. If Tacitus stylistically did not have the same appeal for humanistic scholars as Cicero and Livy, nevertheless his popularity for other reasons was immediately assured. "He supplied texts for every school of political thought, illustrations for every phase of human character. Every class, every people, were able to draw from him maxims which seemed to fit their own case. In every country, at every period, under every variety of political and social condition, men found in Tacitus a mouthpiece for the ideas and feelings of their time."[35]

## CHAPTER VIII

# AMMIANUS MARCELLINUS

THE SPAN of time which separates the historical labors of Ammianus from those of Tacitus was approximately as long as that which lay between the death of Thucydides and the literary activity of Polybius. During the intervening two centuries and a half, historical writings all but disappeared from Latin literature. In the Greek-speaking world they continued with unabated tenacity; the quality of what was written, to judge by what has survived, rarely rose above the mediocre. The periods chosen for treatment were varied. The general history of Rome, contemporary history, and special periods of the more distant past—all had their exponents. Of these Arrian, the historian of Alexander the Great, was the most meritorious, since he shunned the legendary material that had accumulated for centuries and went back to contemporary sources in order to reconstruct the life and achievements of the Conqueror. The study of chronology, too, was not neglected, though its fullest development was only reached when Christian investigators, notably Eusebius, turned their attention to it. Their purpose was twofold: to bring the events of the pagan and the Jewish past into a clearer time relationship, and to establish a satisfactory ecclesiastical calendar in which the movable festivals of the Church could be accurately determined year by year.[1] The use of Greek by literary men whose native tongue was Latin was nothing new. Two of Claudius' books were composed in it; so were several of Suetonius' lost works and the so-called *Meditations* of Marcus Aurelius. But the historians who lived in the age of the Antonines and later all employed their mother tongue; for, although a Dio might settle in Rome, all were natives of the Eastern provinces—Arrian, Dio, and Euna-

[1] For notes to chapter viii, see pages 180–183.

pius from Asia Minor, Appian from Alexandria, Herodian from Syria, Dexippus from Athens. Their labors were a part of that continued though slowly declining florescence of pagan thought and letters to which the Latin-speaking West has no real counterpart to offer. There, after the later second century, most of the significant literature was produced by Christian writers; but as long as they belonged to a persecuted sect they had more pressing problems to engage them than historical inquiry. In pagan circles, historical and even biographical writing, with which we are not here concerned, dwindled away. It produced only epitomes and brief surveys of Roman history, or collections of imperial *Lives*—like the lost compilation of Marius Maximus composed as a continuation of Suetonius, and the still later collection known nowadays as the *Augustan History,* which is by all odds the most contemptible work in all Latin literature.[2]

When the political anarchy of the third century had been ended by the establishment of a more stable, if autocratic, government, literary pursuits even of a modest sort, provided they were harmless, still as in earlier centuries enjoyed a certain degree of patronage from the rulers and might lead to preferment in the imperial service.[3] Clio may have smiled ironically when two of the least of her followers, Eutropius and Aurelius Victor, were thus honored by the imperial favor, while Ammianus Marcellinus, it would seem, reaped only the approbation of his friends and that inner satisfaction which is the true reward of good work well done.

Ammianus, a Greek of good family, was born in Syrian Antioch in or soon after A.D. 330. In early manhood he was accepted into the special military corps of the *protectores domestici,* serving in the mounted section.[4] In 353 he was detailed to join the staff of Ursicinus, then Master of the Cavalry (*magister equitum*). His association with this officer, for whose sterling qualities he conceived a great admiration, seems to have lasted without break for seven years. His duties took him to Italy, to the Rhine, and to Gaul. There he remained until the summer of 357, when his chief received orders to take over the direction of operations on the Eastern frontier. Ammianus has related some of his experiences in this campaign against the Persians with considerable detail, and for the modern reader this personal narrative is one of the "high spots" of his *History*. But he does not tell us what happened to him when, in 360, Ursicinus was superseded in his command. It has generally been assumed, but on quite insufficient evidence, that he remained in Antioch for a spell as a civilian. It is more likely that he continued soldiering; and certainly in 363 he was again on active service on the Eastern front during Julian's last campaign.[5] After that he appears to have returned to civil life. For a time he lived in Antioch; but later on, perhaps soon after 378, he traveled to Rome, where he seems to have resided until his death. How long a time he spent on the composition of his book, when it was completed, or indeed when he died, we do not know.[6] The writing of the *History,* which, as the separate prefaces to Books XV and XXVI suggest, was probably published in parts, perhaps ten Books at a time, would have been a lengthy undertaking even if the author had used his mother tongue. But he chose to write in Latin, and his decision to do so brings to mind an interesting historical contrast.

The greatest of English historians, it will be recalled, began his literary career with an essay, composed in French, on the study of literature; he also experimented with several subjects of historical inquiry before he finally settled on Imperial Rome as his theme. Among these earlier projects was a history of the Swiss wars of liberation. Like his *Essai,* it was written in French, and Gibbon himself relates how the first part was read at a meeting of foreign critics and men of letters in London. "A specimen of my History," he says, "the first book, was read the following winter in a literary society of foreigners in London; and as the author was unknown, I listened, without observation, to the free strictures and unfavourable sentence of my judges. The momentary sensation was painful; but their condemnation was ratified by my cooler thoughts." Even more interesting, however, than this episode is a letter which Gibbon received from David Hume, to whom the manuscript had been shown by their mutual friend, Deyverdun. The letter deserves to be better known than it is, if only for the remarkable prediction that it contains regarding the future diffusion of the English language:

It is but a few days since M. Deyverdun put your manuscript into my hands, and I have perused it with great pleasure and satisfaction. I have only one objection, derived from the language in which it is written. Why do you compose in French, and carry faggots into the wood, as Horace says with regard to the Romans who wrote in Greek? I grant that you have a like motive to those Romans, and adopt a language much more generally diffused than your native tongue: but have you not remarked the fate of those two ancient languages in following ages? The Latin, though then less celebrated, and confined to more narrow limits, has in some measure outlived the Greek, and is now more generally understood by men of letters. Let the French, therefore, triumph in the present diffusion of their tongue. Our solid and increasing establishments in America, where we need less dread the inundation of Barbarians, promise a superior stability and duration to the English tongue.

Your use of the French tongue has led you into a style more poetical and figurative, and more highly coloured, than our language seems to admit of in historical productions; for such is the practice of French writers, particularly the more recent ones, who illuminate their pictures more than custom will permit us.[7]

"More poetical and figurative, and more highly coloured, than our language seems to admit of in historical productions"! In very similar terms some Latin writer, especially if his own style had been formed, like Lactantius' or even Jerome's, in imitation of classical models, might have passed judgment on Ammianus' manner of composition.

His *History,* when complete, covered a period of nearly three centuries, as he himself explains at the end of the work.

I, an ex-soldier and a Greek, have unfolded these events, from the principate of Nerva Caesar to the death of Valens, measuring up to my task as best I could, never wittingly, I think, presuming to disfigure by silence or lie a work which professes to be true. Other, abler men who are in the prime of life and scholars may write the rest. But if it please them and they approach this task, I advise them to shape their tongues to a more elevated style.[8]

It is regrettable that the first thirteen Books have not survived, although they cannot have contained more than a compressed survey of two and a half centuries. In the extant Books XIV to XXXI the scale is quite different, for they describe the events of only twenty-five years, from A.D. 353 to 378. Why did he choose to compose his *History* in Latin, and what was the manner of its composition? There is no certain answer to these questions, but they deserve some consideration.

His Roman patriotism was intense and displayed itself in many ways. He scourges the faults and vices of society in the city of Rome, but Rome herself is "eternal" and "venerable." She is the "home of empire and all the virtues," and her handsome buildings fill him with the same awe and pride that he attributes to Constantius.[9] His Romanism shines through constantly in the military portions of his book, when he comments on the successes and failures of Roman arms; and it is reflected also in his hatred of the Germanic tribes. He reserved the term *barbari* for them, the Alans, and the Huns, and for one or two savage tribes elsewhere; but he never applies it to the Persians, against whom his own fighting was done. His references to them are dispassionate and free from rancor. But the Germans are likened to "wild beasts accustomed to live by pillage when their keepers are off guard"; the Alamanni are an *immanis natio,* and only those familiar with Latin will appreciate the mixture of disgust and

contempt implied by those two words. He even justifies the
treacherous murder of a band of Saxons, after they had been
granted a truce, with the cynical comment: "Granted that an
impartial judge will censure this deed as treacherous and base,
yet, having weighed the matter in his mind, he will not be in-
tolerant toward the destruction, when the means were at last
at hand, of a pernicious band of robbers."[10] Obvious also is his
dislike of barbarian officers in the Roman armies, especially if
they were promoted to positions of great responsibility. Although
the loss of Book I makes it impossible to say how he prefaced his
*History,* his final words imply that it was intended as a continuation of Tacitus—another reason why he chose Latin rather than
Greek as his medium of expression. May one not also suppose
that a man as widely read in Latin literature as Ammianus would
be acutely conscious that, since Tacitus, no historical work of any
scope or signal merit had been composed in that language, and
would be fired with ambition to remedy that lack?[11] Like Tacitus
he narrowly escaped oblivion; it is legitimate to wonder whether,
if he had written his book in Greek, he would have fared better
with posterity which for a thousand years knew him not.

His method of composition has puzzled critics, principally
because they have assumed that Latin always remained something of a foreign tongue to him. He has been said to belong
to Greek rather than to Latin literature.[12] This is as ridiculous a
judgment as if one assigned John Lyly to Spanish literature because the novel style of *Euphues* harks back to Spanish models.
Furthermore, it has been seriously suggested that Ammianus first
composed his narrative in colloquial Latin and then worked it
up into the highly ornate and rhetorical form in which it was
recited to a Roman audience and subsequently published.[13] This
hypothesis argues a singular ignorance of later Latinity; it also
attributes a procedure, which a modern student set to translate
a piece of English into the style of Ammianus might feel it nec-

essary to adopt, to an ancient author who was bilingual, even though he might admit an idiom or turn of phrase characteristically Greek into his Latin. To say that Ammianus learnt his Latin as a soldier is mere assumption; even if true, it is inadequate as an explanation. There was a wide difference between the written and the spoken language and also between the spoken language of the educated and of the uneducated man. One cannot deny that Ammianus is fond of showing off his extensive reading by the introduction of quotations or reminiscences from other Latin authors; but this was fashionable in his day. His thorough familiarity with Latin rhetoric is patent. Thus, one characteristic trait, which is quite in keeping with the fashion then prevalent, is his copious use of historical *exempla* by way of comparison or contrast, not merely in the many digressions in which most of his allusions to the earlier periods of Roman history occur, but in the main narrative. He records, for example, some of the spiteful remarks made at Constantius' court about the Caesar Julian, attributing them to envy; then he enumerates Cimon, Aemilianus, and Pompey as notable men who similarly had been targets for detractors. The treacherous murder of an Armenian king by a Roman commander at a guest banquet gives occasion for recalling the assassination of Sertorius at a feast, and is contrasted with the very different conduct of Fabricius Luscinus, who might have poisoned King Pyrrhus in his cups but instead had warned the king against treachery.[14] The strict differentiation in vocabulary and idiom observed by Cicero and his contemporaries between what was proper in prose and what was admissible only in poetry was already weakening in the Silver Age, as every reader of Livy and Tacitus is aware. This process continued, and the abundant use of poetical words and phrases by Ammianus, though carried to great lengths, was not the mark of a foreigner writing Latin.

It is safe to conclude that Ammianus received a sound training in Latin rhetoric as taught in his day; I myself should go further and maintain that he was as much at home in Latin, when he began his *History,* as Gibbon was at home in French. How he acquired this familiarity with a second language can only be guessed. Since there were certainly facilities for studying Latin rhetoric in Antioch,[15] what more likely than that he had already made some progress before he joined the Guards, and that he took up the subject again with renewed zest after he had returned to civilian life? His style, at least on first acquaintance, may strike one as *sui generis,* but several considerations should deter one from dogmatic pronouncements. Yet such have been made in plenty, often by critics and editors whose knowledge of Latin literature appears not to extend beyond the second century after Christ. It happens that there is no writer contemporary with Ammianus who closely resembles him; but at least in the following century one need only turn to the prose writings of Sidonius, Avitus, or Ennodius, to see a similarly ornate, overloaded manner of expression and a vocabulary largely poetical and shot through with reminiscences from Virgil and others. This highly mannered style may be wearisome and distasteful to a modern reader, but it was greatly admired in the literary circles to which these men belonged; and Latin was the mother tongue of all three. Among Ammianus' Christian contemporaries there is great stylistic variation. To appreciate this fact one need only compare the almost colloquial manner of Ambrosiaster,[16] the semi-Ciceronian style of Jerome, and the copious and involved rhetorical periods of Augustine in his more elaborate treatises.

It is the practice of Ammianus to estimate the character, virtues, and vices of the leading personages in the *History* after he has recorded their death; in this, as in many other ways, he was following the example of Tacitus. The length of these appraisals varies with the importance of the deceased, but when writing of Julian he goes much further than with any other man. He gives an entire chapter to the merits and faults of his hero, and in the earlier part of it adheres closely to the practice of the schools. He enunciates the four cardinal virtues "as defined by philosophers," namely, self-control (*temperantia*), wisdom (*prudentia*), justice (*iustitia*), and courage (*fortitudo*), and adds some other traits—military knowledge, authority, good fortune (*felicitas*), and liberality. Then he applies each of these in order to Julian's character, beginning with his chastity after he became a widower, classifying it as a special type of *temperantia*. One wonders whether Ammianus lays special emphasis on Julian's sexual abstinence in order to show that a virtue which was exalted by contemporary Christian teachers was equally attainable by a pagan and believer in the old religions. However that may be, the whole passage affords unmistakable proof of his rhetorical training, supplemented perhaps by some study of philosophy. At least we know that he had read several of Cicero's philosophical dialogues, and *De officiis* may have been among them.

Surprise has sometimes been felt that he introduced relatively few speeches into his *History,* since there are only twelve in all. To these one may add two letters exchanged between Sapor and Constantius and a long dispatch sent to Constantius by Julian after his proclamation as Augustus by the legions in Gaul. The narrative is also enlivened here and there by short allocutions or conversations, but these never run to more than a few lines." The letters, though reproduced in Ammianus' style, may well be based on official documents. As for the speeches, there is never more than one to a Book; thus their purpose was at once limited. Earlier historians, as we have seen, commonly wrote their speeches in pairs, thereby bringing graphically before the reader the arguments for and against a given policy. It was the logical use of the *genus deliberativum*. Ammianus' procedure was different. Ten of his orations are harangues by emperors to their soldiery, justifying their past actions or conciliating their men. Two of these are very similar in character and situation. In one, Constantius presents the new Caesar Julian to the troops; in the other, it is Valentinian who confers the rank of Augustus on his young son, Gratian, in the presence of the army.[18] The technique employed is the same; each emperor directs the first part of his speech at the military audience, the second part to the person being honored, and what is really a single speech is broken up into two sections by a short piece of narrative describing the response of the audience.

The remaining two speeches are nonmilitary; one is a straight piece of narrative in the first person in which an accused member of the Household Troops confesses to magical practices, the other is the address of the dying Julian to his friends.[19] None of these twelve orations is of great length. There is no effort to characterize the oratorical manner of the speaker; for Ammianus always uses the same rhythmic prose divided into *clausulae* that he employs in the body of the narrative. How far any of them were based on actual speeches it is hard to say. As for Julian's discourse on his deathbed, we may remember that Ammianus was himself participating in the campaign on which Julian was mortally wounded. Though probably not himself present at this moving occasion, he is sure, in view of his profound admiration for Julian, to have inquired from some eyewitness what the last observations of the philosopher-emperor had been. Ibsen, it may be remembered, with poetic license makes the captain Ammian converse with the dying emperor and even puts in Ammian's mouth words that the historian himself attributes to another.[20] The ten military harangues in different ways all impress on the reader one outstanding fact—the ruler's complete dependence for his position on the good-will of his troops. This is not merely the opinion of an ex-soldier, but sober fact. That Ammianus was sparing with speeches because his concept of historical writing differed from that of the other ancients, that, in other words, he consciously disapproved of such fictitious additions to a factual narrative, is most improbable.[21] It is the type of anachronism which even careful scholars sometimes commit when they apply the standards of their own age to the distant past. Ammianus' procedure is susceptible of a simpler explanation. In Sallust, Livy, and Tacitus the speeches, more often than not, are introduced where a discussion in the senate or before the popular assembly is being related. But under the rigid autocracy of the Later Empire the old functions of senate and comitia had completely disappeared. The people did not deliberate and the senate in Rome was hardly more than a town council. The imperial privy council (*consistorium*) was made up of high officials selected by the emperor to be his advisers; to have reproduced any of its deliberations, about which no outsider could have gleaned reliable information, would have been an obvious impropriety and the result would have been devoid of all verisimilitude. And if he had, through a leakage in high places, obtained any confidential news, its publication would have endangered the informant and the historian alike. Thus Ammianus confined himself to simple addresses to the soldiery, a type of speech which earlier historians had also composed from time to time. Such harangues are not easy to classify, but in the main they belong to the *genus demonstrativum*. Here again Ammianus is in line with the tastes of his age; for it was the epideictic speech which was especially popular in Sophistic circles and with the educated public. Finally, many seeming peculiarities in Ammianus' diction can be paralleled elsewhere—an important fact which his various editors have sometimes overlooked when they have introduced unnecessary emendations into his text.[22]

His knowledge of Latin literature was truly remarkable for the age in which he lived, and one can forgive him a certain touch of vanity which at times prompted him to obtrude it. The width of his reading is attested by his constant use of *exempla,* by occasional citations, especially from Cicero and Virgil, and by his vocabulary. Cicero, Livy, and Tacitus among prose writers, Virgil among the poets, are his favorites; but, in addition, there are twenty or more other authors, from Terence to Ausonius, whose phraseology is echoed by him.[23] Although his diffuse manner of writing is so different from the concise style of Tacitus, the influence on him of the older writer was profound. He not only borrows short phrases, but even adopts sentences with slight change, and he imitates Tacitean usages; for example, he writes *ob* instead of *propter,* and he employs simple verbs where those compounded with a preposition might have been expected.[24] But the influence of Tacitus transcended mere linguistic imitations. That the juxtaposition of Constantius and Julian was in some sense inspired by that of Tiberius and Germanicus is perhaps fanciful,[25] but Ammianus' attitude to astrology recalls that of Tacitus. He scoffs at its frivolous misuse, but evidently believed that in proper hands it had scientific value. Tacitus, as we saw, is sometimes skeptical, yet when he relates the friendship of Tiberius and Thrasyllus he writes as though he himself were a believer.[26] Ammianus begins his twenty-sixth Book with a reference to critics who expect the historian to record all kinds of *trivia,* like the emperor's dinner conversation or the names of the persons who waited on the city prefect on New Year's Day. The whole passage echoes like sentiments expressed more than once by Tacitus.[27]

The surviving Books of Ammianus' *History,* save for certain digressions, deal with contemporary events. He was an eyewitness of much that he relates, and he also alludes to the firsthand evidence of others. More than once he puts forward the claim to be considered truthful and reliable; his impartiality, from which lapses are few, shows itself in a determination not to overlook the faults even of those whom, like Julian, he most admires. Thus he writes in one place:

As far as I could search out the truth, I have told what in the course of my life I have been enabled to see or to learn by careful inquiry from eyewitnesses, setting out the various events in order. The rest which the following text will divulge, I shall to the best of my powers deal with even more accurately, since I do not fear objectors to the length of my work as they regard it. Brevity is only praiseworthy when it breaks off ill-timed prolixity without lessening the comprehension of events.[28]

He begins his excursus on Thrace with this comment:

A description of Thrace would be easy, if the pens of earlier authors were in accord; but as their unintelligible variation is useless for a work that proposes to be truthful, it will be enough to disclose what we ourselves remember to have seen.[29]

Speaking of a series of trials for treason held at Antioch, of which he does not recollect all the grim details, he excuses himself with the words: "As the full particulars of what was done have escaped my memory, I shall describe succinctly what I can recall to mind."[30] "But this is shocking," some scientific historiaster of our own day will exclaim. "There must have been an official record of the trial; he should have consulted that." The answer is, of course, that under that iron despotism Ammianus had as much chance of inspecting official documents of state trials as a German scholar in the last decade would have had of perusing the secret archives of the Gestapo. There is no doubt that Ammianus did occasionally inspect official sources of information. When he states that no trustworthy documents about the death of Agnatius existed, the natural implication is that he had searched, but without success. He also alludes in a more general way to archival material and warns the reader against a particular example: the public records and published edicts of Constantius were unreliable, because the emperor had lied about his own achievements.[31]

Oral information derived from reputable informants must have been incorporated by Ammianus in his work to a far greater extent than can now be determined. Here and there he is specific. The confusing military moves and countermoves that preceded the battle of Adrianople were difficult to disentangle and called forth an apology:

As, after a multiplicity of actions, I have reached this point in my story, I implore my readers, if I ever have any, not to demand of me a minutely accurate account of casualty figures that it was quite impossible to obtain. It will be enough to describe in order the high spots (*rerum summitates*), without disguising the truth by any lie, seeing that the recital of historical events at all points deserves simple fidelity to truth.[32]

But he did meet one of the few Roman survivors from the disaster of A.D. 378. This soldier was near by when Valens met his death and gave Ammianus his version of the occurrence. A certain Discenes, tribune and recorder (*notarius*), is quoted for his estimate of the Persian casualties at Amida. When the attendants of Constantius and persons close to Julian are cited as authorities for a particular statement, it is presumably because Ammianus had spoken to one or the other himself.[33]

Ammianus does not designate the published histories or narratives that were at his elbow when he composed the extant portions of his *History*. The truth seems to be that for these contemporary events there was little that he could have consulted. He may have made use of the Latin *Annals* by Flavius Nicomachus. This cannot be satisfactorily demonstrated, but in view of his wide reading it seems to be inherently probable. The hypothesis that for his account of the Persian campaigns he relied on the diaries of Magnus of Carrhae, and that in general he consulted an anonymous Greek writer whose narrative is supposed to have been arranged by summers and winters after the manner of Thucydides, rests on no sound basis of evidence.[34] In the many digressions Ammianus was considerably indebted to earlier authorities. He mentions Timagenes, the contemporary of Augustus, as his chief guide when he was composing his lengthy description of the Gauls.[35] These excursuses have brought him censure from some of his modern critics on account of their length and irrelevance and the interruptions that they cause in the main narrative; but it is quite unfair to lump them all together in this way.[36] Some, like that on obelisks or on eclipses of the sun and moon, are perhaps dragged in without adequate reason and could well be spared. But the geographical descriptions of Gaul, of the Hellespont and Black Sea, of Thrace, and of the Persian provinces were justifiable in themselves. Nor would one be without the description of the Huns, perhaps the most widely known passage in Ammianus' book.[37] One may admit that he has not exercised sufficient care or restraint in these parts of the *History*. He mixes up facts or scientific data with mythology, not so much because he believes these fictions, but because for the moment the rhetorician in him is stronger than the historical inquirer. And even though some of his facts can be shown to be erroneous, many of the digressions are "highly interesting and valuable."[38] The well-known description of Rome in the later fourth century, though brilliant, is very rhetorical and to be received with great caution.[39] The theme of *degeneratio* was, as we have seen repeatedly, a favorite one in the schools. At the same time, twelve to fifteen years of soldiering may have given Ammianus a certain distaste for ostentation and luxury as found in the capital cities, especially when this was accompanied by hero worship of Julian and admiration of Julian's austere mode of life.[40] Ammianus' great Christian contemporary, St. Jerome, also fulminated against the Roman manners of his day. The two men could have met in Rome or possibly in Antioch.[41] Walter Savage Landor missed a golden opportunity when he omitted to compose an Imaginary Conversation on the sins of society between the soldier-historian and the Christian ascetic!

As a military historian Ammianus is uneven. Where his narra-

tive is based on personal experience, the topographical information and the operations are clear and intelligible; where he is
dependent on others, there is a tendency toward vagueness of
detail. Also, as with other Roman historians, the pattern learned
in the schools of rhetoric obtrudes itself and darkens, if it does
not obliterate, the individual features of landscape, engagement,
or siege." A good example of a personal narrative, which has the
same lively quality that we find in much of Xenophon's *Anabasis,* is his account of how he escaped after the loss of Amida:

As the evening grew dark, when a large body of our troops, though
unjust Fortune was still fighting against them, were still closely engaged, I with two others hid in a remote part of the town. Protected
by the dark night, I slipped out of a side gate which was left un-
guarded, and, thanks to my familiarity with desert territory and the
speed of my comrades, finally reached the tenth milestone. There at
the posthouse we took a brief rest. As we prepared to push on and
I was all but overcome by too much marching (to which being of good
family I was unaccustomed), I was confronted with a shocking sight,
though it afforded me timely relief when I was utterly tired out. A
soldier servant riding a runaway horse without saddle or bit, to pre-
vent his slipping off, had tied the bridle rein, by which in the usual
way he was guiding the animal, too tightly to his left hand. Presently,
being thrown and unable to break the knot, he was torn limb from
limb as he was dragged along over trackless places and through brush-
wood, until the beast, tired out with galloping, was stopped by the
weight of his corpse. I caught the horse and opportunely used the
service of its back, and with the same companions barely reached some
springs of sulphurous water warmed by nature. Parched with thirst
because of the heat, we crawled on a long while in search of water,
when luckily we spied a deep well. But owing to its depth we could
not go down into it, and we had no ropes with us. So, taught by extreme necessity, we tore up the linen clothes that we were wearing
into long strips and twisted these into one long rope. To the end of it
we fastened the cap which one of us wore under his helmet and let it
down by the rope. When it was saturated with water like a sponge, it
easily quenched the thirst that consumed us. From this point we

pushed on quickly to the Euphrates, meaning to cross to the farther side in a boat kept in that region for daily use, to ferry men and cattle across. But lo! from a distance we espied a Roman column with cavalry standards all in disarray and pursued by a great force of Persians; but we were in doubt from what quarter they had suddenly come up behind us in their march. With this example before me, I believe that the Earth-born men did not spring out of the bowels of the earth, but came to birth with exuberant speed. Then, as they appeared unexpectedly in various places, they got the name Sparti, and were believed to have leaped out of the ground; for antiquity elevated the occurrence into a myth. Aroused by the sight of the Persians, as our only assurance of safety lay in haste, we made off for the high mountains through brush and forest. Then from there we reached Melitine in Lesser Armenia, where presently we found and accompanied our commanding officer, who was on the point of departure, and returned unexpectedly to Antioch.[43]

The passage affords an excellent illustration of Ammianus' manner. The main story is well told, but he cannot resist the temptation of slipping in a pompous phrase here and there, to say nothing of the farfetched rationalization of a myth. Similarly, after relating vividly enough how he and a centurion had been sent on a secret mission to the friendly governor of Gordyene, and had actually witnessed from rising ground the Persian army as it crossed the river, he ends rhetorically with an allusion to the hosts of Xerxes in 480 B.C.:

How long, O Greece, lover of tales, wilt thou tell us of Doriscus, the Thracian town, and of the armies led regiment by regiment into pens and counted, when we cautious or, to speak more truly, timid historians will overstate nothing beyond what has been established by reliable and sure proofs?[44]

Seeck was right when he praised highly Ammianus' powers as a narrator and his skill at characterization, qualities for which he was not wholly unworthy to be named in the same breath as Tacitus.[45] But there is another quality in which he surpasses the older writer—his conspicuous fair-mindedness. Apart from his undisguised dislike of Germans, he displays an obvious bias in only two passages of his *History*. One of these is the description of Roman society, which is a kind of satire inspired by a long-established literary tradition and perhaps by the rigors of his earlier life; the other is a bitter outburst near the end of the work, against the whole tribe of lawyers.[46] Was this invective, with its elaborate division into four types of "violent and greedy classes of men, who flit from court to court, lay siege to wealthy homes, and, like Spartan or Cretan hounds, sagaciously follow up the scent until they arrive at the very lairs of lawsuits," and its exhaustive use of rhetorical artifice, inspired merely by certain general notions aroused by observing frequent malpractices in the administration of justice? It may be so, but it is tempting to imagine that behind his vitriolic bitterness lay some personal experience of having been bested by a smart attorney. For the rest, Ammianus' love of truth and fair judgment carry the day. He is judicial, as we saw, in summing up the good and bad in his leading characters. Himself a pagan, he is free from animus against the Christians and even blames Julian for legislating against them. He passes an unfavorable judgment on Athanasius as a meddler given to exalting himself above his station, but at the same time admits that he is repeating persistent rumors, and also that Constantius was always the bishop's enemy; and he obviously feels respect for Liberius, who objected to condemning a man unheard. A notable passage suggests that Ammianus was writing from his own knowledge and observation when he praised "certain provincial bishops, whose extreme frugality in eating and drinking, simple dress, and eyes fixed earthward commend them as pure and reverent men to the eternal divinity (*perpetuo numini*) and his true worshipers." He contrasts their simplicity with the luxurious mode of life customary among prelates in Rome, and records with evident disapproval the factional fights in that city caused by the rivalry of Ursinus and Damasus.[47] Some have praised him for his spirit of toleration, others have explained his attitude as indifference. The former estimate is the fairer. Although his own religious beliefs were not inspired by implicit faith in any one cult or doctrine, but show some fluctuation, he was not an atheist, nor even an agnostic. He inclines to monotheism in the language that he uses most often, his practice being to speak of *numen,* as in the passage just quoted, with some suitable adjective (*supernum, caeleste, sempiternum*) appended. His conformity with the ritual requirements of the old pagan state religion seems to have been lukewarm; and on two occasions he reprehends Julian for his undue addiction to sacrifices and his excessive trust in omens and portents, calling him "superstitious rather than a legitimate observer of sacred rites."[48] But then, there was nothing of the mystic in Ammianus as there was in Julian, whose religious enthusiasm was the least Hellenic thing about him. As the most penetrating of Julian's modern biographers has observed: "Au IVe siècle, jusque dans les milieux les plus hostiles à la religion nouvelle, on était sous son influence, et lorsque l'Apostat subissait l'ascendant de Maxime d'Ephèse, il y avait, dans son enthousiasme, un fanatisme étranger à l'esprit hellénique dont il se croyait pénétré."[49] Elsewhere Ammianus himself relates supernatural phenomena without evincing any skepticism. His attitude to astrology has already been noted, and at times he is frankly a fatalist. Dreams and other means of foretelling future events evidently impress him, and he ends a discussion of this topic by appealing to the authority of Cicero: "The gods show signs of coming events. If a man is mistaken in these, it is not the nature of the gods but the human interpretation that is faulty."[50] Ensslin, in the course of a long and careful analysis of Ammianus' beliefs, is disposed to lay great emphasis on certain passages which he thinks suggest the influence on the historian of Neoplatonic doctrines.[51] He may be right; but there is always a danger in labeling

as Neoplatonic beliefs or opinions which by the fourth century
were not peculiar to Plotinus and his followers, but rather had
become the common property of pagan thought on philosophy
and religion. Ammianus nowhere betrays that he knew or was
influenced by that part of Neoplatonism which was essentially
its own. He is, in short, no philosopher. The uncertainty of his
convictions and a certain groping after truth stamp him as a
normal representative of educated paganism in its decline.

Those historians, from Gibbon to the present, who have
studied the Later Empire, are agreed in extolling the merits of
Ammianus. We owe to him our clearest picture of two great
forces set over one against the other—Rome senescent, but, thanks
to Diocletian and his successors, still retaining some of her
pristine vigor and tenacity, and the Germanic peoples on her
northern frontiers or even within her very borders. Ammianus
is not blind to the heavy price that the citizens of the Empire were
paying for a security that was steadily becoming more precarious.
Knowing his rhetorical manner, we might be tempted to assume
that the oppression of the common man and the harsh judicial
measures and savage punishments, which shock his humanity
and ours, are overdrawn—a terror imagined and portrayed by
an admirer and imitator of Tacitus. But it was not so. Ammianus'
narrative is often highly colored, but its essential truth is proved
by comparing it with the Theodosian Code, that grim collection
of ordinances and rescripts from Constantine to Theodosius II
and unimpeachable record of iron regimentation and merciless
penalties, designed to intimidate or coerce the nonconformist.
Furthermore, Ammianus' own love of letters and culture is genuine and deeply rooted; it is not a personal vanity. For him the
older civilization of Rome and all it stood for is contrasted with
the rude illiteracy of her northern neighbors; for him it is the
spiritual, as the Roman armies are the physical, bulwark against
advancing barbarism. We may freely grant that his understand-

ing of the fourth century and of the world-shaking movements that were under way was in many respects defective; yet what he has recorded is a true if incomplete presentation of the times through which he lived. The eulogy which Bidez has pronounced over him as the biographer of Julian belongs to him of right as the historian of the later fourth century.[52] In the temple of Clio his place is by the side of Livy and Tacitus.

# NOTES

## LIST OF ABBREVIATIONS

| | |
|---|---|
| *AJP* | *American Journal of Philology* |
| *CP* | *Classical Philology* |
| *CQ* | *Classical Quarterly* |
| *CR* | *Classical Review* |
| *F Gr Hist* | *Fragmente der griechischen Historiker*, ed. F. Jacoby. In progress |
| *FHG* | *Fragmenta historicorum graecorum*, ed. C. Müller (Paris, 1841–1851) |
| *HRR* | *Historicorum romanorum reliquiae*, Vol. I, ed. H. Peter (2d ed.: Leipzig, 1914) |
| *JRS* | *Journal of Roman Studies* |
| *RE* | *Realencyclopädie der klassischen Altertumswissenschaft*, ed. Wissowa-Kroll-Mittelhaus. In progress |
| *TAPA* | *Transactions of the American Philological Association* |

# NOTES

## CHAPTER I

### THE HELLENISTIC BACKGROUND

#### (Pages 1–22)

[1] The usual word for chronicler in the inscriptions is ἱστοριογράφος. Cf. W. Dittenberger, *Orientis Graeciae Inscr.* 13, 12 (3d cent. B.C.); idem, *Sylloge Inscr. Graec.*[3] 560, 13; 685, 93; 702, 3 (2d cent. B.C.); *Greek Inscr. in the British Museum* III, 1 (from Samos). On one of these chroniclers, Syricus of Chersonesus, and his relation to the Lindus chronicle from Rhodes, see M. Rostovtzeff in *Klio* 16 (1920), pp. 203–206.

[2] Polyb. i.4.3; Diod. i.3, whose ideas in the opening chapters of his work are derived in the main from Posidonius.

[3] Aelian iii.18.

[4] Diodorus, to whom we owe this information, is not free from obscurity. Cf. the useful discussion in G. L. Barber, *The Historian Ephorus* (Cambridge, Eng., 1935), p. 17.

[5] Cf. André Aymard, *Les Premiers Rapports de Rome et de la confédération achaienne* (Bordeaux, 1938), *passim*; C. F. Edson, Jr., in *Harvard Studies in Classical Philology* 46 (1935), pp. 191–202.

[6] R. Laqueur in *RE*, s.v. Timaeus; Cicero, *De nat.* ii.69.

[7] *F Gr Hist* 76 F 1.

[8] Polyb. ii.56.

[9] E. L. Woodward, *War and Peace in Europe, 1815–1870, and Other Essays* (London and New York, 1931), p. 188.

[10] *Saturday Review* 17 (1864), p. 81.

[11] Aristotle, *Poet.* (tr. S. H. Butcher) 1451a–b.

[12] *Ibid.* 1459a, reading καὶ μὴ ὁμοίας ἱστορίαις τὰς συνθέσεις. The text in this passage has been a matter of dispute for centuries, but the arguments of A. Gudeman in his recent edition of the *Poetics* (p. 388) in favor of this reading seem incontrovertible.

[13] *Rhet.* 1393a (tr. Lane Cooper).

[14] Cf. Paul Scheller, *De hellenistica historiae conscribendae arte* (Diss. Leipzig, 1911), or a more recent writer who says of the Peripatetic or "tragic" style of writing history: "Ihre Eigenart ist in der Uebertragung der aristotelischen Lehre und Vorschriften vom Drama auf die Historiographie begründet; ihre theoretische Formulierung erfuhr sie wahrscheinlich zuerst durch Theophrast oder seinen Schüler Praxiphanes." See Erich Burck, *Die Erzählungskunst des T. Livius* (Berlin, 1934), p. 176. The sanest presentation of the case for a "tragic" style of historical writing is the article, "History and Tragedy," by B. L. Ullman, in *TAPA* 73 (1942), pp. 25–53.

[15] Xen., *Hellen.* ii.3.

[16] *Ibid.,* iv.5.4–7.

[17] Polyb. xii.28.10. Unhappily, he does not tell us whether Ephorus' γνωμολογίαι dealt with persons or situations, or possibly with both. Examples of his digressions

are to be found in x.43 (Fire signals), xviii.18 (Making palisades), and iv.38–42 (The Black Sea and the natural advantages of Byzantium).

[18] T. Carlyle, *History of Frederick the Great*, Book XVI, chapter 10 (Vol. IV, p. 318), in the library edition published in 1905 by Chapman and Hall). Cf. also the interesting remarks, based on his experience as editor of the *Dictionary of American Biography*, of Mr. Dumas Malone in *The Interpretation of History* (ed. J. R. Strayer; Princeton, 1943), pp. 121–148.

[19] Sir Charles Firth, in his posthumously published *Commentary on Macaulay's History of England* (London, 1938), pp. 37–38, draws attention to Macaulay's device of the "declamatory disquisition" which fulfilled a function similar to that of the speeches in the ancient historians.

[20] Cicero, *Brut.* 11.43, ". . . mortem rhetorice et tragice ornare potuerunt."

[21] Though composed more than half a century ago, R. von Scala's *Die Studien des Polybius* (Stuttgart, 1890) is still valuable to anyone interested in the formation of Polybius' mind.

[22] In xxix.21 Polybius refers to Demetrius by name and cites a fairly long passage from him *verbatim*.

[23] E.g., i.63.9; ii.38.5.

[24] *Ibid.*, i.4.1.

[25] Diod. i.1.3 (tr. C. H. Oldfather). Cf., in general, Karl Reinhardt, *Kosmos und Sympathie* (Munich, 1926), pp. 184–185.

[26] *F Gr Hist* 87 F 36. Reinhardt, *op. cit.*, p. 386, observes of Posidonius as a historian: "Vielleicht war überhaupt sein Werk mehr Sitten-, Zeit-, und Weltgemälde als eine pragmatische Geschichte—in historischer Form eine Art comédie humaine." It is an attractive hypothesis but quite unsusceptible of proof.

[27] Thus Chrysippus (*Stoicorum veterum fragmenta* 939) accepted divinations only so far as they were in harmony with the predestined order: Μὴ γὰρ ἂν τὰς τῶν μάντεων προρρήσεις ἀληθεῖς εἶναι φησίν, εἰ μὴ πάντα ὑπὸ τῆς εἱμαρμένης περιείχοντο.

[28] Seneca, *Epist.* 90.6, ". . . subrepentibus vitiis in tyrannidem regna conversa sunt."

[29] The interested reader should turn for a fuller discussion of these theories to R. Hirzel, Ἄγραφος νόμος (Abhandlungen der sächsischen Gesellschaft der Wissenschaften, Phil.-hist. Klasse, 1900), pp. 78–98; and to Waldemar Graf Uxkull-Gyllenband, *Griechische Kultur-Entstehungslehren* (Bibliothek für Philosophie, 26. Band; Berlin, 1924), who maintains that Posidonius tried to reconcile orthodox Stoic teaching of a Golden Age with an evolutionary theory (Aszendenstheorie) derived from Protagoras and Democritus.

## CHAPTER II

### ROMAN HISTORIANS TO THE DEATH OF CAESAR

#### (Pages 23–44)

[1] The phrase and the classification are the late Tenney Frank's in the *American Historical Review* 32 (1927), pp. 232–240. Strangely enough, save for one brief mention, he ignored Cato's *Origines*.

[2] *HRR*, Asellio, fr. 6; Sallust, *Iug.* 95.2.

[3] There is nothing to prove that the distinction drawn by Verrius Flaccus (A. Gellius v.18.1) between *annales* and *historia* ever passed into common usage. According to this theory, "annals" dealt with the past, "history" with contemporary events. To Cicero the distinction was clearly one of literary form, not content. To him all the earlier writers of history were *non exornatores sed tantummodo narratores* (*De leg.* i.5). Livy avoided both terms; Tacitus so far agreed with Verrius as to call the book which dealt with events of his own lifetime *Historiae*. His so-called *Annals*, however, he himself designated *ab excessu divi Augusti libri XVI*. Mr. Lloyd Daly in his recent article, "The Entitulature of Pre-Ciceronian Writings" (*Classical Studies in Honor of W. A. Oldfather* [Urbana, 1943], pp. 20-38), has brought together a most useful collection of data which prove great variation in the use of the words *annales* and *historia*. But when he observes (p. 24), "In any case there seems to be no effort to distinguish works in accordance with the fundamental meaning of the two words," and refers to Gellius and Servius in a footnote, he assumes that Verrius' definition was "fundamental." All the evidence that he has brought together proves the contrary—that there never was a general agreement about the two words in the Roman writers. The *ipse dixit* of a professor, then as now, was insufficient to establish a linguistic usage!

[4] Cicero, *Brutus* 14.54 ff.

[5] The hypothesis of R. C. W. Zimmermann (*Klio* 26 [1935], pp. 260 ff.) that Fabius' command of the Greek language was due to his descent from a Greek ancestor who had been a freedman and client of an earlier Fabius is ingenious but highly speculative. Analogies are dangerous, especially between ancient and modern times; but certainly in the United States and in Great Britain it is unusual for the first generation of native-born children to command the language of their immigrant parents well enough to write it fluently and idiomatically. For the second or even third generation to remain bilingual must be exceedingly rare.

[6] *HRR*, Cato, fr. 49 contains an allusion to the war with Perseus and must therefore have been written after 168 B.C. Frs. 106-109 concern the prosecution of Galba for his conduct as praetor in Spain in 149.

[7] *HRR*, Cato, fr. 45; cf. 31.

[8] *HRR*, Cato, fr. 83 relates the heroism of Q. Caedicius in the First Punic War. Fr. 95 preserves a part of Cato's speech delivered in the senate at the time of the Rhodian debate in 167. Cato, at least in his later books, was contemptuous of the information sometimes included in annals; cf. fr. 77.

[9] *HRR*, Fabius, fr. 24. Cf. also H. N. Wethered, *The Mind of the Ancient World* (London and New York, 1937), p. 87.

[10] *HRR*, Cato, frs. 39, 97, and 110.

[11] *HRR*, Fabius, frs. 3 and 15; Gellius, fr. 21; Coelius, frs. 11, 20, 34, 49, and 50; Sisenna, fr. 5. But Sisenna at the same time expressed his own opinion that no belief should be placed in dreams. Cicero attributes this skepticism to Epicurean influence, and another fragment (123) suggests this also.

[12] *HRR*, Claudius, fr. 78, *equae hinnibundae inter se spargentes terram calcibus*. For Claudius' style cf. frs. 10b, 57, and 81.

[13] There has been a tendency to follow Mommsen's lead, who judged Licinius severely because he was influenced by Livy's comment (viii.9.1) that the annalist

liked to exalt members of the *gens Licinia*. But so sound a scholar as Münzer (*RE*, s.v. Licinius, no. 112) credits the annalist with a genuine desire to add to the knowledge of early Roman history by using long-neglected records.

[14] *HRR*, Asellio, fr. 1.

[15] Fr. 8.

[16] *HRR*, Claudius, frs. 40–41; Antias, fr. 21. The story had a long history; cf. Peter's note on the Claudius fragments.

[17] *HRR*, Antias, fr. 25. Mr. Dumas Malone (*The Interpretation of History*, pp. 134–135) in an interesting passage points out how the efforts to blacken the character and private life of Thomas Jefferson can be traced back to a single hostile journalist.

[18] *HRR*, Antias, fr. 48 and the list of references given in Peter's note. To these may be added an allusion in the ninth-century commentator on St. Matthew, Christian of Stavelot, who had found the story in Jerome. See my article in *Harvard Theological Review* 20 (1927), pp. 135–136 with note 23.

[19] Cicero, *De divin.* i.49. *HRR*, Cato, fr. 2 with Peter's note. For Timaeus' influence on Fabius and Cato cf. Werner Schur in *Klio* 17 (1921), pp. 137–143. R. Laqueur (*RE*, s.v. Timaeus, col. 1203) makes the not improbable suggestion that Polybius, when he criticized Timaeus (Pol. xii.26d3) for having led other authors astray with his foundation legends, was tacitly alluding to Cato's *Origines*.

[20] For Italia derived from ἰταλοί (= *vituli*) see Timaeus in *FHG* I, fr. 12 and *HRR*, Piso, fr. 1.

[21] Fabius' estimate had the approval of Cato and Polybius. Cf. generally *CP* 3 (1908), pp. 316–329.

[22] Cicero, *De orat.* i.34.158; i.60.256; ii.15.62.

[23] *Ibid.*, ii.13.55.

[24] Cicero, *De leg.* i.5. A few scholars have pointed out the true meaning of this passage, but their remarks have usually been ignored. See G. Boissier, *Tacitus and Other Roman Studies* (tr. W. G. Hutchinson; New York and London, 1906), pp. 46–47, and A. Gwynn, *Roman Education from Cicero to Quintilian* (Oxford, 1927), pp. 106–107. In a book published as recently as 1938 the old misinterpretation reappears; cf. K. Barwick, *Caesar's Commentarii und das Corpus Caesarianum* (*Philologus*, Supplementband XXXI, 2), p. 124.

[25] Cicero, *Brutus* 16.62; Livy viii.40.

[26] Cicero, *Ad fam.* v.12; for Cicero's request to Posidonius cf. *Ad Att.* ii.1.2. The translation of part of Cicero's letter is by W. Glynn Williams (Loeb Classical Library).

[27] The earliest extant work which is autobiographical in content, though not in form, is Isocrates' speech, *On the Exchange of Property*, published in 354–3 B.C.

[28] Plutarch, *Marius* 26.

[29] See especially T. Rice Holmes, *Caesar's Conquest of Gaul*[2], pp. 211–256. This is a masterly book to which all students of Caesar must of necessity be greatly indebted. See also the briefer discussions in Holmes's *Roman Republic* II, pp. 334–337 and III, pp. 382–383. One of the most conspicuous merits of Holmes, who could argue about historical *minutiae* with the best of them, was that he never allowed his discussion of controversial matters to obscure the over-all view of his subject. He at least always had the forest, not merely the trees, before his mind's eye.

[30] The case for separate publication of the seven Books has most recently been presented by Karl Barwick in the book cited above. He gives extensive references to the earlier literature on the subject. There is uncertainty also about the date of publication of the *Commentaries on the Civil War*. The common view, which depends in part on the interpretation of the phrase *confecto bello* (iii.57.5 and iii.60.4), is that the book was not published until after the battle of Munda in 45 B.C., or even posthumously after Caesar's death, with the added implication that it was an *opus imperfectum*. But *bellum* may not mean the whole of the Civil War; indeed, in the context in which the words occur they are more likely to refer to that phase of the war which ended with Pompey's defeat at Pharsalus and subsequent murder in Egypt. In that case, the work might have been published at any time after 48 B.C. That Cicero in the *Brutus*, which appeared in 46, mentions only the *Gallic War* proves nothing either way. Considering his political sympathies, we may feel sure that he would in any case have passed over Caesar's later work in silence. Barwick, however, has argued (*op. cit.*, pp. 165–171) not without some plausibility that the three parts of the *Civil War* were issued piecemeal, I and II after Ilerda but before Caesar left Italy for Epirus, III in 47 B.C.

[31] Pollio's estimate is preserved in Appian ii.82. It should be noted that Caesar in estimating the casualties of his opponents' army is by no means positive in his statement; for he writes (*B. C.* iii.99), "ex Pompeiano exercitu *circiter* milia xv cecidisse *videbantur*."

[32] *B. C.* iii.111.

[33] For the correct meaning of *constratae* see T. Rice Holmes, *Roman Republic* III, p. 441, note 5.

[34] *B. C.* iii.68.1.

[35] *Ibid.*, 70. So also in iii.27, it was a lucky chance that the wind shifted, making it possible for Antony to land in Epirus and so to bring much-needed reinforcements to his chief.

[36] *Ibid.*, iii.15.

[37] *Ibid.*, iii.18.

[38] *Ibid.*, ii.42.

[39] *Ibid.*, iii.43. Actually there are ninety-nine words in the Latin text, or, if *que* be counted as a separate word, one hundred and three. On Caesar's style and Latinity cf. the judicious appraisal by W. H. Alexander in *University of Toronto Quarterly* 12 (1943), pp. 415–425.

[40] *B. C.* i.72.

## CHAPTER III

### SALLUST

#### (Pages 45–64)

[1] Sallust, *Hist.* iv, fr. 77.

[2] Cf. M. R. James, *The Ancient Libraries of Canterbury and Dover* (Cambridge, Eng., 1903), p. 9, nos. 94–101.

[3] Loup de Ferrières, *Correspondance* (ed. L. Levillain; Paris, 1935), II, p. 124.

[4] Werner Schur, *Sallust als Historiker* (Stuttgart, 1934), pp. 13 ff. Though he lists the more important German scholars since Jordan who have discussed the *Suasoriae*,

he ignores the important contribution to the subject by Hugh Last in *CQ* 17 (1923), pp. 87–100, 151–162; 18 (1924), pp. 83–84. Last makes out a strong case for rejecting as spurious the *Suasoria* standing second in the manuscripts; he concludes that the first is quite possibly genuine. My own belief is still that the older editors were right in regarding both as rhetorical forgeries. There is a very recent discussion of the evidence in *Latin Pseudepigrapha* by E. H. Clift (Baltimore, 1945), pp. 107–113. Miss Clift thinks both *Suasoriae* and also the *Invective against Cicero* are Sallustian. There is this at least in favor of the *Invective*, that Quintilian believed in its authenticity. Schur passes it over in silence, presumably because it would not readily fit into his highly imaginative reconstruction of the growth of Sallust's mind. One may also point out that he is writing strongly under the influence of current political theories as understood in Germany. Cf., for example, the amusing estimate of Lucullus (Schur, *op. cit.*, p. 279): "Auch er war doch bei aller politischen Kraft und Energie, die er *gegen die demagogischen Umtriebe* in seinem Konsulatsjahr bewiesen hat, und bei aller militärischen Befähigung *keine Führernatur, wie sie der schwerkranke Staat brauchte.*" The italics are mine.

⁵ The edition by Wasse is very valuable for the many examples that it contains of echoes in Sallust from Greek literature. Among recent books Kurt Latte's *Sallustius* (Leipzig, 1935) is useful in this regard. It is also marked by a sanity of outlook that contrasts strongly with the phantasies of recent Sallustian studies in Germany. The copy of Wasse's book in the library of the University of California at Berkeley once belonged to Edward Gibbon and bears his bookplate.

⁶ Cf. Thucydides iii.40 with *Cat.* 7.5; Thuc. iii.82 with *Cat.* 41 and 62.1. In *Cat.* 59.5 the picture of Petreius riding round and calling his veterans individually by name is borrowed from Thucydides' account (vii.69) of Nicias at the siege of Syracuse.

⁷ The echoes in Sallust from Plato's *Seventh Epistle* and from the *Olynthiacs* are well known. *Hist.* i, fr. 88 is indebted to Demosthenes' picture of Philip II in *De corona* 67. With *Jug.* 85.49 cf. *Menexenus* 247D. Karl Münscher in *Xenophon in der griechischen und lateinischen Literatur* (*Philologus*, Supplementband 13[1920]), pp. 82–83, implies that only the *Cyropaedia* and the *Memorabilia* were familiar to Sallust and his Roman contemporaries. But *Jug.* 14.1 clearly recalls the words of Clearchus in *Anabasis* i.3.6, while the grim phrases in which Sallust describes a battlefield after the battle was over (*Jug.* 101.11) imitate the description of the field of Coronea in *Agesilaus* 2.14.

⁸ With the passage in *Jug.* 85.34, "his ergo praeceptis milites hortabor neque illos arte colam, me opulenter, neque gloriam meam laborem illorum faciam," one may compare what Isocrates (*Helen* 36) says of Theseus: οὐ γὰρ ὥσπερ ἕτεροι τοὺς μὲν πόνους ἄλλοις προσέταττε, τῶν δὲ ἡδονῶν αὐτὸς μόνος ἀπέλαυεν, ἀλλὰ τοὺς μὲν κινδύνους ἰδίους ἐποιεῖτο, τὰς δὲ ὠφελείας ἅπασιν εἰς τὸ κοινὸν ἀπεδίδου. Other possible echoes of Isocrates occur in *Cat.* 2 (cf. *Areopag.* 4); *Cat.* 7.4 (cf. *Areopag.* 48). Catiline's list of the horrors incidental to revolution (21.2) resembles *Panathenaicus* 259 and also Demosthenes, *De corona* 15.

⁹ Cf. T. R. S. Broughton in *TAPA* 67 (1936), pp. 34–46.

¹⁰ *Cat.* 4.2; *Hist.* i, fr. 6.

¹¹ Cf. *HRR*, Sisenna, fr. 127 and Sallust's *Histories* (ed. Maurenbrecher), p. 57.

[12] *Hist.* i, frs. 4 and 5. I assume that fr. 5 refers to Cato, but this is not certain.

[13] *Jug.* 95.2.

[14] Manlius' dispatch is introduced (*Cat.* 32.3) with the words: "legatos ad Marcium Regem mittit cum mandatis *huiuscemodi.*" But of Catiline's letter it is said (34.3), "earum (i.e., litterarum) *exemplum* infra scriptum est."

[15] Suetonius, *De gramm.* 10.

[16] Cf. *Cat.* 19.5, 22.4, 48.9, where Sallust alludes to what Crassus had said at a later date than the conspiracy.

[17] *Hist.* ii, fr. 98, "scelestissimi hostes" (cf. *Hist.* iv.69.2); "totiens fuso sanguine" (cf. *Jug.* 106.3, "totiens fusum Numidam"); "studio maiore quam consilio" (cf. *Hist.* ii, fr. 64, "studio maiore quam opibus").

[18] Cf. Plato, *Phaedo* 80A; *Gorg.* 465D (εἰ μὴ ἡ ψυχὴ ἐπεστάτει τῷ σώματι); Aristotle, *Pol.* 1254a34; Isocrates, *Antid.* 180 and 253 ff.; *Nic.* 5 ff.

[19] *Iug.* 1.5; Herod. vii.49.

[20] *Hist.* i, frs. 12 and 16.

[21] The antitheses in Sallust (*Cat.* 2; *Jug.* 4; *Hist.* i, frs. 11 and 12) between *luxuria, avaritia, superbia, ambitio, desidia,* and *continentia, aequitas, probitas, industria,* had become hackneyed long before his time. Thus in Isocrates (*Areopag.* 4) ἄνοια and ἀκολασία which attend wealth and power are contrasted with σωφροσύνη and μετριότης which go with frugality and lowliness. In pseudo-Demosthenes, *Epitaph.* 2, wealth and luxurious pleasure are opposed to ἀρετή and the desire for good fame. Hyperides (*Epitaph.* 5) in a striking metaphor compares the sun which fosters life and growth with the Athenian state which punishes the bad and protects the just and assures for all equity in place of ambition and greed (πλεονεξία).

[22] *Cat.* 12.3–4; Demosthenes, *Olynth.* 3.26; c. *Aristocr.* 207.

[23] *HRR,* Piso, fr. 40, "queritur adulescentes *peni* deditos esse," with which cf. *Cat.* 14.2, "manu, ventre, *pene* bona patria laceraverat." Lucil. (ed. Marx), 1326.

[24] Cf. H. von Fritz in *TAPA* 74 (1943), pp. 134–168. Polybius in one passage (ii.21.8) dates back the beginning of the degeneration of the people to the agrarian legislation of Flamininus in 232 B.C.!

[25] Much of the evidence for Sertorius has reached us indirectly, coming from Plutarch's *Life,* for which Sallust was the chief source. The very unfavorable estimate of Sertorius put forward by H. Berve (*Hermes* 64[1929], pp. 99 ff.) is an excellent example of misplaced ingenuity characteristic of that writer. It has been criticized by M. Gelzer in *Philologische Wochenschrift* 52 (1932), pp. 1129–1136, and refuted by Schur, *op. cit.,* pp. 223–256.

[26] See K. Cichorius, *Römische Studien* (Stuttgart, 1922), pp. 172–174.

[27] Cf. T. R. S. Broughton in *TAPA* 67 (1936), p. 45.

[28] Polybius xxiii.12 ff.

[29] *Jug.* 93 ff.

[30] Cf. Maurenbrecher's note on *Hist.* ii, fr. 87.

[31] Schur, *op. cit.,* p. 139.

[32] Quintilian x.1.102.

[33] *Hist.* ii, fr. 70 and ii, fr. 87.

[34] *Cat.* 52; *Jug.* 85.

[35] *Hist.* i, frs. 55 and 77; ii, fr. 47; iii, fr. 48.

³⁶ "On pourra souscrire au jugement de Carolsfeld (p. 78) que le discours de Philippe est le chef d'œuvre de Salluste, puisque l'auteur a abandonné sa propre diction et s'est assimilé complètement celle de l'orateur," Ragnar Ullmann, *La Technique des discours dans Salluste, Tite Live, et Tacite* (Oslo, 1927), p. 42. Cicero's estimate of Philippus is in *Brutus* 173. Mr. Ullmann has failed to see how Sallustian the phraseology of the speech is, as some examples will demonstrate: "Bellum ex bello serunt" (cf. *Hist.* iv, fr. 69, "bella ex bellis serendo"); "qui peior an ignavior sit, deliberari non potest" (cf. iv, fr. 1, "perincertum solidior an vanior"); "quam maturrime" (cf. i, fr. 66, "maturrime"); "si tanta torpedo animos obrepsit" (cf. iii, fr. 48, "verum occupavit nescio quae vos torpedo").

³⁷ Thus in the edition by B. Ornstein and J. Roman (*Collection Budé;* Paris, 1924) the pages bearing the Latin text are nearly always shorter by several lines than the pages of the translation.

³⁸ Cf. the interesting remarks on French imitators in the Introduction of the edition cited in the preceding note.

## CHAPTER IV

### LIVY, THE MAN AND THE WRITER

#### (Pages 65–82)

¹ Francis Bacon, *The Advancement of Learning*, ch. 2.

² For a more appreciative estimate of Cicero by Pollio cf. Seneca, *Suas.* vi.24. B. L. Ullman in *TAPA* 73 (1942), pp. 50–51, would classify Pollio's *History* "among the monographs written in tragic fashion," but there is no satisfactory evidence for this. Mr. Ullman's case rests entirely on a questionable interpretation of Horace, *Odes* ii.1. The supposed parallels in expression between Cicero in his letter to Lucceius and Horace prove nothing, because they are quite general, and the phrases describing the uncertainties and vicissitudes of fortune are rhetorical commonplaces. The interpretation of Horace's lines, "paulum severae musa tragoediae desit theatris" as "Pollio will return to the writing of *tragedy* when he has finished his *tragical* history" reads into them something that is not there and ignores what follows in the poem. Horace alludes clearly to the three fields of literature at which Pollio had tried his hand—tragedy, history, and oratory; and that is all.

³ Valerius was quoted by authors of the first and second centuries A.C.; cf. *HRR* I, pp. cccxxviii ff., and also Tenney Frank, *Life and Literature in the Roman Republic*, p. 187.

⁴ It would be difficult to cram more nonsense into one sentence than has been done by Schanz-Hosius, *Geschichte der römischen Literatur* I, p. 318: "Livius hat ihn (i.e., Valerius) in seiner Kritiklosigkeit nicht weniger als 35-mal zitiert; freilich auch ihm sind die Augen aufgegangen, und nicht selten hat er dann seinem Aerger Luft gemacht." The fact that Livy usually refers to Valerius by name in order to differ from him is proof of the precise opposite to an uncritical attitude. Moreover, Livy's eyes were wide open from the beginning; for he alludes to Valerius already in the first decade (iii.5.12) and his use of the word *audet* implies a direct criticism of his source.

⁵ Cf. above, p. 28.

[6] For an unbiased estimate of Valerius see A. A. Howard in *Harvard Studies in Classical Philology* 17 (1906), pp. 161–182. This article is still worth careful study.

[7] Strabo v.C213 and 218; H. Dessau, *Inscr. latinae selectae* 5406.

[8] Livy iv.6.12 and x.2.

[9] *Ibid.* xli.27.3; Plutarch, *Caesar* 47; Cicero, *Phil.* 12.10; Macrob. *Sat.* i.11.

[10] The hypothesis was put forward by W. B. Anderson in his edition of Book IX, appendix (3d ed.; Cambridge, Eng., 1934).

[11] Seneca, *Epist.* 100.9. The elder Seneca records an unfavorable judgment passed by Livy on Sallust and a criticism of orators who employ obsolete words and colloquialisms and confuse a plain with an obscure manner of writing. Quintilian relates that Livy alluded to a rhetorician who encouraged his pupils to compose in an obscure manner; he also mentions a letter written by Livy to his son. Cf. Livy (edd. Weissenborn-Müller [Bibliotheca Teubneriana, ed. stereotypa]), frs. 73–76. Since nothing remains of these works, it is immaterial whether Livy's *obiter dicta* were to be found in the compositions mentioned by the younger Seneca or in some other work devoted to writing and style. Livy's contemporaries, like posterity, thought of him as the historian of Rome.

[12] Livy viii.6.3; xxiv.10.6; xxvii.37.1, *ibid.* 32.2: xliii.13.1.

[13] Cicero, *De divin.* i.127.

[14] Cf. the careful analysis of Livy's speeches in the monograph by Ragnar Ullmann to which reference has already been made. As for the first reservation made in the text, a good example of unsound method will be found in C. N. Cochrane, *Christianity and Classical Culture* (Oxford, 1940), p. 101. Mr. Cochrane speaks of "Livy's professed belief in the Stoic dogma of an immutable fate" and in support cites one passage, xxv.6. But the phrase occurs in the speech of one of the survivors from Cannae. The allusion to destiny is entirely appropriate to the character of the speaker and need not apply to Livy himself at all. Mr. Cochrane would have done better to quote a passage like viii.7.8.

[15] xlii.47.9, "vicit tamen ea pars senatus, cui potior utilis quam honesti cura erat."

[16] v.19.8; ix.17.3.

[17] xliv.40.3; cf. fortuna in v.37.1.

[18] i.4.1; v.36.6; viii.7.8; ix.33.3; i.7.11 and 15.

[19] Livy, *Periochae* 48, 49, and 50.

[20] Seneca, *Suas.* vi.

[21] An extreme example of this type of reasoning is to be found in Kahrstedt's chapter in O. Meltzer und U. Kahrstedt, *Geschichte der Karthager* (3 vols.; Berlin, 1879–1913), III, pp. 143 ff.

[22] Livy (i.19.3) alludes to the closing of the temple of Janus in 27 B.C. and to the final pacification of Spain in 19 B.C. (xxviii.12.12). Augustus' legislation of 18 B.C. is mentioned in *Periocha* 59. In the standard text edited by Conway and Walters each volume that has appeared to date contains five Books of Livy. The number of pages varies between 400 and 460, but much of the space on each page is taken up by variant readings, so that 300 pages of continuous text seems a reasonable estimate.

[23] The handicaps under which an ancient historian worked are well stated by H. Bornecque, *Tite Live* (Paris, 1933), p. 79, but for the reasons stated in the text they should not be given too much weight.

²⁴ Sixty-two Books (lxxii–cxxxiii) for sixty-two years (91–30 B.C.), but the scale is not quite uniform. The revolutionary period from 91 to 79 filled eighteen Books, and the civil war period, 50 to 30 B.C., twenty-five. The intervening twenty-nine years were described in nineteen Books.

²⁵ Pliny, *Nat. hist.*, pref. 24.

²⁶ *Periocha* 69.

²⁷ *Periocha* 88.

²⁸ *Periochae* 117 and 130.

²⁹ Seneca, *Suas.* vi.22.

## CHAPTER V

### LIVY, THE HISTORIAN

#### (Pages 83–102)

¹ It is usual to cite Kühner-Stegmann, *Ausführliche Grammatik der lateinischen Sprache* II, i, p. 87, in support of the assertion, but not one of the examples there quoted of the rhetorical plural is an accurate parallel to Livy's use of *auctores*. Among those who have protested against this so-called *Einquellenprinzip* are A. A. Howard in *Harvard Studies in Classical Philology* 17 (1906), p. 180, and H. Peter, *Die geschichtliche Literatur über die römische Kaiserzeit* (Leipzig, 1897), II, pp. 264 ff.

² Livy xxxiv.15.10; xxxviii.23.6; Klotz in *Hermes* 50 (1915), pp. 529 ff.

³ Livy ii.40.10; xxii.7.3; Tenney Frank in *JRS* 9 (1919), pp. 202–207, and in *Life and Literature in the Roman Republic* (Berkeley, 1930), pp. 195–196.

⁴ Livy's appreciation of Polybius has recently been pointed out afresh by E. K. Rand, *The Building of Eternal Rome* (Cambridge, Mass., 1943), p. 41, note 14. Mr. Rand has treated J. W. Duff with more gentleness than he deserved.

⁵ Cf. xxi.38.2; xxv.39.12; xxvi.49.1; xxxv.14.5; xxxix.52.1.

⁶ These expressions have been analyzed by R. B. Steele in *AJP* 25 (1904), pp. 15–44, and in even greater detail by Fritz Hellmann, *Livius-Interpretationen* (Berlin, 1939), pp. 8–22.

⁷ Livy vi.1.12. He has often been criticized for failure to use the *Fasti Capitolini;* but, as Miss Lily Ross Taylor has recently shown (*CP* 41 [1946], pp. 1–11), they were probably not compiled until Livy had finished at least the earlier decades of his *History*.

⁸ The introduction of a treaty text in Book V and of the agreement between Sparta and Persia in Book VIII has been used, in consequence, as an argument that Thucydides did not revise these sections before publication.

⁹ Cf. Rand, *op. cit.*, p. 41, note 15; Livy iv.7.12.

¹⁰ xxiii.19.8; xli.28.8; viii.10–11.1.

¹¹ viii.40.4; cf. also above, p. 32.

¹² *Advancement of Learning*, ch. 2.

¹³ On this topic see especially W. B. Anderson in his edition of Book IX (3d ed.; Cambridge, Eng., 1934), pp. 161 and 198. There are passages in Livy's narrative which with only slight change can be turned back into hexameter verse. W. Aly in *Ennius und Livius* (Leipzig, 1936) devotes a whole monograph to Livy's study of the poet. The parallels quoted are not always convincing; still, Aly succeeds in

establishing Livy's thorough familiarity with Rome's first national epic. His later book, *Titus Livius* (Frankfurt a. M., 1938), is beneath contempt. It is a thinly disguised Nazi pamphlet which begins with a quotation from *Mein Kampf*.

[14] Cf. the comments of T. R. Glover, *Herodotus* (Berkeley, 1924), pp. 78–85, with an interesting example showing how a popular tradition about John Bunyan, which had been denied by many critics, was ultimately proved correct.

[15] Livy xxxvii.48.7.

[16] xliv.22.6–15.

[17] "Nemo tam famae contemptor est." I think that Livy is playing on the double meaning of *fama*, rumor and personal reputation.

[18] xxvi.22.14.

[19] xxxi.44.3 and 9; viii.22.8; xxxvi.17.5.

[20] xxxii.20.3–4.

[21] vi.20.5.

[22] iv.6.11.

[23] Cf. Hugh Last in *JRS* 35 (1945), pp. 30–48.

[24] *Proceedings of the Classical Association* 34 (London, 1937), pp. 7–28.

[25] Cicero, *pro Balbo* 53; *de rep.* ii.54, with which cf. Livy vii.17.12. Cicero had undoubtedly studied the XII Tables for himself. Strabo I, p. 67, Ῥωμαίους καὶ Καρχηδονίους οὕτω θαυμαστῶς πολιτευομένους.

[26] So good a scholar as M. Cary (*History of Rome*, p. 48, note 20) says of Cicero's summary of early Roman history: "Cicero's narrative is very competent as far as it goes."

[27] H. Bornecque, *Tite Live*, pp. 88–89. It is a pity that his otherwise admirable essay is marred by such hypercriticism.

[28] Ragnar Ullmius, *La Technique des discours dans Salluste, Tite Live, et Tacite*, pp. 17–18, "Tite Live ne réussit pas à s'émanciper de l'école et à peindre d'après la vie." R. M. Henry, *op. cit.*, p. 23, speaks of "lay figures clothed in abstract virtues, not living characters who left behind them a tradition of their personality." "Quantum mutatus ab illo!" In an earlier work, his edition of Book XXVI (London, 1905), Mr. Henry showed sounder judgment. On p. xii he remarked: "How well, for instance, is Scipio's character sketched in a few slight strokes in the speech he delivers to his soldiers before the start from New Carthage, and again with consummate skill in the short speech to Aluccius after the capture of the town; we see Scipio's whole character bared before us *votiva veluti descripta tabella*."

[29] Livy xl.9–15; xxviii.39; xlv.41.

[30] Ragnar Ullmann, *op. cit.*, pp. 17–18. Mr. Ullmann's analysis of Livy's speeches is valuable, but his classification seems to me too rigid. Their general plan and the balance of their parts are not as uniform as he would have us believe. He even proposes to deduce from the arrangement of the speech whether Livy adhered closely to his source or not. "Ainsi," he says, "que nous pouvons établir la thèse que dans Tite Live c'est un indice de sa dépendance de la source s'il compose ses discours d'après les règles de la rhétorique en détail ou non." It is a pity that he has spoiled a learned and helpful monograph by extravagances of this sort—the result of overmuch preoccupation with German "Quellenforschung."

[31] Cf., for instance, E. Burck, *Die Erzählungskunst des Livius*, p. 135; M. Cary,

*History of Rome*, p. 71. The suggestion that Livy had Augustus in mind when he portrayed a man like Camillus has most recently been made by F. Hellmann, *Livius-Interpretationen*, p. 54.

[32] Livy vii.2; ix.30; x.23; xxvi.13–14; xl.4.

[33] ix.30; Ovid, *Fasti* vi, 657 ff.; Plutarch, *Roman Questions* 55. See also W. W. Fowler, *The Roman Festivals* (London, 1908), pp. 157–159.

[34] xxvii.50.

[35] G. Becker, *Catalogi bibliothecarum antiqui* (Bonn, 1885), No. 70, 46: "Libri 10 Livii ab urbe condita, sed capita XL adhuc desunt Pomposiano abbati, quae reperire avide anhelat."

[36] The epitomators of Livy have been discussed by Marco Galdi in an able essay published in *Studi liviani* by the Istituto dei studi romani (Rome, 1934).

## CHAPTER VI

### TACITUS AND HIS FORERUNNERS

#### (Pages 103–122)

[1] Students interested in this question should consult the admirable article, "The Decay of Eloquence at Rome," by Harry Caplan in *Studies in Speech and Drama in Honor of A. M. Drummond* (Ithaca, N. Y., 1944), pp. 295–325. As Mr. Caplan points out (p. 323), other causes for decline were named by the ancient writers, but the main stress is laid on autocracy and its effect on the freedom of the individual.

[2] Quintilian, *Inst. orat.* x.1.102 ff. Cordus' book was burnt, but some copies survived and were reëdited in the time of Caius. For the evidence cf. E. Groag et A. Stein, *Prosopographia imperii romani*, ed. 2, II, No. 1565.

[3] Tacitus, *Hist.* i.1 (tr. G. G. Ramsay).

[4] Pliny, *Epist.* v.8.12.

[5] Bassus has been the subject of detailed study by F. A. Marx. See his articles in *Klio* 26 (1933), pp. 323–329; 29 (1936), 94–101 and 202–218. Though some of his conclusions are very speculative, he has made it probable that Bassus' works were a favorite quarry for later authors.

[6] Suetonius, *Claud.* 41–42; Tacitus, *Ann.* xi.14. Cf. also A. Momigliano, *Claudius: The Emperor and His Achievement* (Oxford, 1934), p. 10.

[7] Velleius ii.1. De Quincey's essay will be found in Vol. X of the *Collected Works*, edited by David Masson (Edinburgh, 1890).

[8] Velleius i.16–17.

[9] *Ibid.* ii.89. Even the eulogy of Sejanus is understandable, since Velleius knew him merely as a good soldier and administrator. Besides, at the time when the compendium appeared, Sejanus was still the trusted minister of Tiberius.

[10] Cf. *Prosopographia imperii romani*, ed. 2, II, No. 1467. There is some uncertainty about Tacitus' praenomen. It is given as Publius in the margin of the first Medicean codex, while Sidonius twice calls him Caius.

[11] Tacitus, *Hist.* iii.1.

[12] Pliny, *Nat. Hist.* iv.102 ff.

[13] Tacitus, *Agr.* 14, 21, 27, 30.

[14] The allusion of St. Jerome (Migne, *Patrologia latina* 25, col. 1522D) to the thirty

Books in which Tacitus described the lives of the Caesars has been much discussed. If the *Annals* were complete in eighteen Books, the *Histories* on his reckoning must have been in twelve. In that case the scale on which the later Books of the *Histories* were composed must have been appreciably smaller than that of the surviving four and a half Books. Since for the reign of Domitian Tacitus had no predecessor to consult, but had to gather all his own material, he may have decided on a briefer treatment than in the early Books where he still had Pliny the elder as a guide.

[15] Tacitus, *Ann.* ii.65.1; iv. 33.2.

[16] *Agr.* 42.5; *Hist.* iii.51.

[17] So F. Klingner in *Die Antike* for 1932, p. 168: "Die Gedanken des Tacitus bewegen sich letztlich immer um eine Stelle, wie um ihren Pol, um die altrömische *virtus*, den Inbegriff allen Wertes, der der mit Schmerz und Stolz geliebten römischen Welt innewohnt." Klingner makes no mention of H. Peter, *Die geschichtliche Literatur über die römische Kaiserzeit* II, p. 46, who had expressed substantially the same view in less flowery language. In order to bolster up his theory Klingner also proposes to date the *Dialogus* in the opening years of the second century. But he gives no adequate reasons for this. Nor does he find it necessary to explain why Tacitus, at a time when he was engaged on the *Histories* and had evolved his mature and characteristic style, should in the *Dialogus* relapse into a quasi-Ciceronian manner.

[18] R. Reitzenstein, *Tacitus und sein Werk* (*Neue Wege zur Antike*, Heft 4, 1925).

[19] Notably by J. Vogt, *Tacitus als Politiker* (Stuttgart, 1924).

[20] See M. Rostovtzeff, *Social and Economic History of the Roman Empire* (Oxford, 1926), p. 86, and F. B. Marsh, *The Reign of Tiberius* (Oxford, 1931), p. 14.

[21] R. von Pöhlmann, "Die Weltanschauung des Tacitus," in *Sitzungsberichte der k. bayerischen Akademie*, 1910: Phil.-hist. Klasse, Abhandlung 1. Cf. p. 63: "Was man so gewöhnlich die 'Weltanschauung' des Tacitus nennt, ist ein Chaos von unabgeklärten und unausgereiften Meinungen, ein Sammelsurium von Widersprüchen, zwischen denen eine Ausgleichung unmöglich ist. Auch kann man nicht sagen, dass die eine oder die andere dieser Meinungen irgendwie dominierend in den Vordergrund trete, wie etwa bei Seneca. Die Möglichkeit eines rein natürlichen Pragmatismus sind mindestens ebenso ernstlich, wenn nicht ernstlicher erwogen, als die eines mystisch-religiösen. Mit grossartiger Offenherzigkeit hat er den ganzen Zwiespalt, der seine Seele erfüllte, die innere Zerrissenheit seines Denkens in die Darstellung selbst hineingetragen und vor den Augen des Lesers enthüllt."

[22] Tacitus, *Ann.* vi.22.1. At the end of the chapter he refers to dishonest astrologers and adds: "ita corrumpi fidem artis, cuius clara documenta et antiqua aetas et nostra tulerit."

[23] Cf. *Ann.* iv.20.5; *Hist.* i.10 and i.18.

[24] For Fortuna cf. *Hist.* ii.1, iv.47; *Ann.* iv.1, xvi.1. For contempt of superstition see *Hist.* ii.1, iv.26; *Ann.* xiii.58. One may contrast with these passages others as in *Ann.* xii.43; xii.64; xv.7.

[25] *Hist.* ii.38.

[26] *Ann.* iv.1.3; xvi.16; xvi.33.2.

[27] The attribution of the various speeches in the *Dialogus* is not free from uncertainty. I have used the text in the latest edition of the Bibliotheca Teubneriana.

[28] *Agr.* 2.

²⁹ A similar technique is used by Tacitus in *Ann.* xvi.25–26 to represent the varying advice tendered to Thrasea.

³⁰ *Ann.* iii.28.3–4.

³¹ E. K. Rand, *The Building of Eternal Rome*, pp. 162–165, sees in Tacitus a monarchist, "if monarchy means Ideal Empire, founded on law and harmony and peace." But Mr. Rand omits in his translation the passage referring to the Poppaean Law, and also glosses over the essential point when he reverses the order of the words, *pace et principe*: "give us laws whereby we might enjoy our princely ruler and our peace."

³² Cf. *Ann.* xiii.20; xiv.2; xv.53; xv.61. Pliny the elder is also named in *Hist.* iii.28 and, specifically for his work on Germany, in *Ann.* i.69. Messalla is mentioned twice in the *Histories* (iii.25 and 28).

³³ *Ann.* iv.53; xv.16.

³⁴ *Ann.* xv.74.3.

³⁵ Marsh (*op. cit.*, pp. 274 ff.), for example, is cautious, although he inclines to credit Tacitus with considerable familiarity with the *acta*. F. A. Marx in *Klio* 29 (1936), p. 97, tacitly assumes an extensive and direct use of them. E. Ciaceri, on the other hand, after stating his reasons, sums up categorically (*Tiberio* [Milan, 1934], p. 65): "È chiaro che Tacito non aveva direttamente esaminati gli Atti del senato e che solo li aveva conosciuti di seconda mano."

³⁶ Cf., for instance, *Ann.* iv.10, v.9, xiii.17; *Hist.* ii.101. On the danger of rumors see *Ann.* iii.16; xi.27; xv.41.

³⁷ *Ann.* iv.11, xi.27.2.

³⁸ Pliny, *Epist.* v.5 and viii.12.

³⁹ See F. A. Marx, "Tacitus und die Litteratur der exitus illustrium virorum," in *Philologus* 92 (1937), pp. 83–103. According to H. Peter (*op. cit.*, I, p. 185), these writings were fostered by senatorial opponents of the principate.

## CHAPTER VII

### TACITUS, THE HISTORIAN

#### (Pages 123–140)

¹ On the literary ancestry of the famous phrase, *sine ira et studio*, see the note by B. L. Ullman in *Classical Journal* 38 (1943), p. 420.

² *Hist.* iii.33, 82–85.

³ *Hist.* i.86.

⁴ *Ann.* i.76 and 79.

⁵ See chapter vi, note 39, above.

⁶ *Hist.* i.41.

⁷ *Hist.* iii.84–85.

⁸ Livy xxxi.18.6–7; Polybius xvi.34.9–10. The extreme restraint of Thucydides is well known. A conspicuous example of it is his reference to the death *by torture* of Aristogeiton: ὕστερον ληφθεὶς οὐ ῥαδίως διετέθη (vi.57).

⁹ *Hist.* ii.76–77; iv.73–74.

¹⁰ Tacitus' speech is in *Ann.* xi.24. The text of the Lyons inscription will be found in Furneaux's edition of the *Annals*, II, pp. 56–60, and in M. P. Charlesworth,

*Documents Illustrating the Reigns of Claudius and Nero* (Cambridge, Eng., 1939), pp. 6 ff.

[11] See E. Hohl in *Klio* 32 (1939), pp. 307–324; Suetonius, *Otho* 8.2.

[12] The example of unsound method criticized in the text will be found in P. S. Everts, *De tacitea historiae conscribendae ratione* (Diss. Utrecht, 1926). This writer is also obsessed with the "tragic" style of historical composition.

[13] On the recitation of Tacitus' works in Rome cf. the illuminating remarks of G. G. Ramsay, *The Annals of Tacitus*, II, pp. lxxv ff.

[14] *Ann.* iv.3.3–4; vi.49.1; xi.21.

[15] Furneaux, *Annals of Tacitus*, I, p. 29.

[16] *Ann.* iv.6.

[17] *Ann.* vi.5–6.

[18] *Ann.* i.76.6–7.

[19] E.g., *Ann.* iii.53–54; iii.69.

[20] *Ann.* iv.38.4–6.

[21] *Ann.* vi.51.5–6.

[22] Cf., for example, F. B. Marsh, *op. cit.*, pp. 200 ff., 216, and on the provinces, pp. 134 ff., although this part of the book could have been amplified by more archaeological evidence; M. P. Charlesworth, *Harvard Theological Review* 29 (1936), pp. 110–112 and 124–125, as well as his chapter on Tiberius in the *Cambridge Ancient History*, Vol. X. Above all, the excellent book by R. S. Rogers, *Studies in the Reign of Tiberius* (Baltimore, 1943), deserves careful study. The modern literature on the reign of Tiberius is enormous but of unequal value. The interested reader should consult the important review-article by Vincent Scramuzza in *AJP* 65 (1944), pp. 401–409.

[23] *Ann.* xii.1.1.

[24] For Claudius' letter to the Alexandrians see H. I. Bell, *Jews and Christians in Egypt*, or M. P. Charlesworth, *Documents*, pp. 3–5.

[25] G. G. Ramsay, *The Annals of Tacitus*, II, p. 108, note 1.

[26] *Ann.* iv.18.3.

[27] *Ann.* iv.33.6.

[28] *Ann.* xv.21.4.

[29] *Ann.* xvi.18.

[30] *Hist.* ii.5.

[31] E. K. Rand, *The Building of Eternal Rome*, pp. 164–165, note 79.

[32] F. B. Marsh, *op. cit.*, p. 14.

[33] The story is told in *Script. Hist. Aug.*, Tacitus 10; but E. Hohl has shown (*Klio* 11 [1911], p. 303; *Hermes* 55 [1920], pp. 300–301) that it is almost certainly spurious.

[34] Cf. the doctoral dissertation, of which two copies are available in the Cornell University Library, by Mary F. Tenney, *Tacitus in the Middle Ages and in England to about the Year 1650* (1931). A summary of her conclusions has appeared in *University of Colorado Studies* 22, no. 4 (1935). The article (*JRS* 6 [1916]) by F. Haverfield is superficial and very incomplete. On a manuscript of the *Agricola* at Monte Cassino in the twelfth century see H. Bloch in *CP* 36 (1941), pp. 185–187.

[35] G. G. Ramsay, *op. cit.*, I, p. xix.

[1] For the evolution of ecclesiastical calendars see the admirable treatment in C. W. Jones, *Bedae opera de temporibus* (Cambridge, Mass., 1943), pp. 6 ff.

[2] Even if the *Historia Augusta* was propaganda disguised as biography, it is still a wretched piece of literature. The reader interested in the controversies about the *H.A.* should consult the brilliant analysis of Norman H. Baynes, *The Historia Augusta: Its Date and Purpose* (Oxford, 1926). Mr. Baynes's main conclusions were accepted by the last and best editor of the text, Ernst Hohl. See *Classical Review* 41 (1927), pp. 82–83. I have not yet seen W. Hartke's monograph, *Geschichte und Politik im spätantiken Rom* (*Klio*, Beiheft 45 [1940]), which offers a fresh discussion of the *Historia Augusta*.

[3] Cf. Otto Seeck, *Geschichte des Untergangs der antiken Welt*, II (ed. 2; Stuttgart, 1922), pp. 189–194, but the whole chapter in which this passage occurs is still well worth study. For imperial patronage of rhetoricians cf. the recent article by W. H. Alexander in *Transactions of the Royal Society of Canada*, Third Series, Sec. II, Vol. 38 (1944), pp. 37–57. On the epitomators and chroniclers of the fourth and fifth centuries cf. my article in *CP* 35 (1940), pp. 241–258.

[4] On the *protectores* see Ernst Stein, *Geschichte des spätrömischen Reiches* I (Vienna, 1928), p. 82 with note 1.

[5] The assumption that Ammianus was not on active service between 359 or 360 and the beginning of 363 is based on the fact that he does not use the first person plural in his narrative between xix.8.12 and xxiii.5.7. Chapter viii of this book had already been written when I gained access to the important article by E. A. Thompson in *Hermathena* 49 (May, 1942), pp. 44–66. For the point here under discussion cf. his Appendix, pp. 64–66. That Ammianus did not go to Rome till after 378 is also a guess, based on his statement that he had visited Thrace and the field of Adrianople. It is assumed that he traveled overland from Antioch to Rome and passed through Thrace on the way.

[6] The latest event recorded by Ammianus is the consulship of Neotherius in 391 (xxvi.5.14). A letter written in 391 by Libanius (*Epist.* 983) alludes to the historian's success at Rome, presumably when he read a portion of his book in public. But the arguments in favor of the assumption that the *History* was finished in 393 seem to me very flimsy. For these see W. Ensslin, *Zur Geschichtschreibung und Weltanschauung des Ammianus Marcellinus* (*Klio*, Beiheft 17; Leipzig, 1923), p. 9; Ernst Stein, *op. cit.*, p. 332.

[7] *The Autobiographies of Edward Gibbon*, ed. by John Murray (London, 1897), p. 277 with note. Hume's letter is No. 412 in *The Letters of David Hume*, ed. by J. Y. T. Greig (Oxford, 1932). Gibbon himself makes a number of acute observations on the use of Greek by Roman, and of French by English, writers.

[8] xxxi.16.9.

[9] xiv.6.5; xvi.10.13; xvi.14–17.

[10] xvi.5.16; xxviii.5.7 and 4.9.

[11] Ensslin (*op. cit.*, p. 10), who is followed by Mr. Rolfe in his edition of Ammianus (I, p. xix) in the Loeb Classical Library, says that Ammianus wrote for Romans in general, and in particular for the literary coterie of which Symmachus was the head. This puts the cart before the horse. If his primary purpose was to write for that *cercle intime*, he could not have decided to write in Latin until after he came to Rome. In view of his wide reading and the long preparation that it necessitated, this seems to me impossible. I should assume that he fixed on Latin as soon as ever he decided to write.

[12] The assertion made by Wilamowitz—a typically dogmatic pronouncement—is quoted by Ensslin (*op. cit.*, p. 30), but is not approved by him.

[13] So W. Klein, *Studien zu Ammianus Marcellinus* (*Klio*, Beiheft 13; Leipzig, 1914), p. 9, note 1. Mr. Rolfe (*op. cit.*, I, p. xx) considers Klein's view "plausible."

[14] xvii.11.2 ff.; xxx.1.22–23.

[15] Libanius (ed. Förster, I, p. 193, 6) alludes to the official appointment of a Latin and a Greek rhetor in Antioch when he says: ἐχθρός τε ἦν καὶ ἐπειρᾶτο τἀμὰ καθελεῖν, πρῶτα μὲν Ἰταλῶν φωνῇ, μετὰ ταῦτα δὲ καὶ Ἑλλάδι. Doubtless there were private teachers of Latin rhetoric in Antioch even earlier. See in general the excellent remarks of Ensslin, *op. cit.*, pp. 35 ff.

[16] "It is fairly obvious that the author cannot have had what we should call a rhetorical training," is the comment of Alexander Souter, *The Earliest Latin Commentaries on the Epistles of St. Paul* (Oxford, 1927), p. 84. See also the remarks of the same writer, the greatest living authority on Patristic Latin, regarding the differences, not only in theological terms, but in language and style, of the Christian writers in the third and fourth centuries (*A Study of Ambrosiaster* [Cambridge, Eng., 1905], pp. 147–148).

[17] G. B. Pighi in his study, *I discorsi nelle storie d'Ammiano Marcellino* (Pubbl. della università Cattolica del Sacro Cuore, Vol. XXIII [Milan, 1936]), pp. 30–31, classifies these short passages in *oratio recta* into a separate group of *discorsi minori*; but they are much too brief to fall under the heading of speeches composed according to strict rhetorical rules. The whole of M. Pighi's monograph is curiously lacking in substance.

[18] xv.8.5–14; xxvii.6.6–13.

[19] xxix.1.29–32; xxv.3.15–20.

[20] See *Emperor and Galilaean*, Part II, Act V, Scene 4.

[21] For this view cf. Ensslin, *op. cit.*, p. 17. On p. 19 he seems to imply that Ammianus abandoned speeches after he had finished Book xxvi. But this is wrong; there are speeches at xxvii.6.6–13 and xxix.1.29–32.

[22] See numerous examples, which can be readily located by reference to the index in each volume, given by Einar Löfstedt in his three works, *Philologischer Kommentar zur Peregrinatio Aetheriae, Syntactica*, and *Vermischte Schriften*. Cf. also G. B. A. Fletcher in *AJP* 58 (1937), pp. 392 ff.

[23] For numerous Virgilian reminiscences, which suggest that Ammianus knew much of the poet by heart, see especially Harald Hagendahl, *Studia Ammianea* (Diss. Upsala, 1921). For other authors cf. the article, "Stylistic Borrowings and Imitations in Ammianus Marcellinus," by G. B. A. Fletcher in *Revue de Philologie* 11 (1937), pp. 377 ff. Mr. Fletcher records a long list of passages noted by himself.

They supplement in a remarkable way the findings of earlier investigators whose books and articles are indicated by him for each author used by Ammianus. In *Philologus* 91 (1936), p. 478, he sets out ten verbal parallels between Ammianus and Solinus, supplementing the examples noted by Mommsen in the second edition of his Solinus.

²⁴ See Einar Löfstedt, *Philologischer Kommentar*, p. 219, for *ob* instead of *propter* in Tacitus and Ammianus. For simple in place of compound verbs in the two authors cf. Löfstedt, *Vermischte Schriften* (Lund, 1936), p. 119 with note 2: "Auch sonst hat Amm. manche Verba simpl. statt der Komposita gebraucht. Zum Teil ist er wohl bewusst den stilistischen Normen des Tac. gefolgt." For a good example of "borrowing" a whole sentence we may compare the opening words of xxii.1.1, "Dum haec in diversa parte terrarum Fortunae struunt volubiles casus," with Tacitus, *Hist.* ii.1, "Struebat iam Fortuna in diversa parte terrarum initia causasque imperio."

²⁵ The comparison is made by Eduard Norden, *Antike Kunstprosa* II, p. 646.

²⁶ Contrast xxviii.4.24 with the respectful manner in which he refers to astrologers in Chaldaea and Alexandria (xxii.16.17 and xxiii.6.25).

²⁷ See especially *Annals* xiii.81, as well as other passages collected by H. Peter, *Geschichtliche Litteratur* II, p. 45 with note 1.

²⁸ xv.1.

²⁹ xxvii.4.2.

³⁰ xxix.1.24.

³¹ xxviii.1.30 ff.; xxviii.1.15; xvi.12.69–70.

³² xxxi.5.10.

³³ xxxi.13.6; xix.9.9; xxi.14.2; xxv.2.3.

³⁴ W. Klein, *op. cit.*, pp. 42 ff., gave special attention to the problem of sources, stressing particularly Ammianus' supposed debt to Magnus of Carrhae. His theories, which already had aroused the skepticism of Richard Laqueur (*RE*, s.v. Magnus von Carrhae), have now been refuted by E. A. Thompson in *Hermathena* 59 (May, 1942), pp. 44–64.

³⁵ xv.9.2.

³⁶ Eduard Norden (*Antike Kunstprosa* II, p. 647) is unjustifiably severe; but his whole treatment of Ammianus is exaggerated. His dogmatic pronouncement about Ammianus' Latin—he speaks of his "Unfähigkeit . . . sich in korrektem Latein auszudrücken"—is surprising from so eminent and usually fair-minded a scholar. It is particularly out of place in view of his admission (p. 646) that he had only read a small portion of the writer whom he criticizes! H. Peter (*Geschichtliche Litteratur* II, p. 128) also condemns the digressions, but Ensslin (*op. cit.*, pp. 15–16) shows more discrimination.

³⁷ Certain phrases in this passage are almost identical with what Ammianus had already said about the Saraceni (cf. xxxi.2.10 with xiv.4.3). They are, in fact, part of the stock description applicable to any nomadic tribe.

³⁸ Cf. Ramsay in W. Smith, *Dictionary of Greek and Roman Biography*, s.v. Ammianus.

³⁹ xiv.6.

⁴⁰ Note the admirable remarks of that sound scholar and discriminating critic,

Sir Samuel Dill, in his *Roman Society in the Last Century of the Western Empire* (London, 1898), pp. 103–104.

[41] St. Jerome was in Antioch in or about A.D. 374; he was back in Rome between 382 and 385. Cf. F. Cavallera, *Saint Jérôme: sa vie et ses œuvres* (Louvain and Paris, 1922), II, pp. 12–22.

[42] Thus the topography of the battle of Strasbourg is still a matter of controversy. Cf. Ernst Nischer in *Klio* 21 (1927), pp. 391–403. The account of the siege of Aquileia (xxi.12.4–20) is one of Ammianus' most graphic pieces; but, though it has plenty of individual and particular features, which he may have obtained from a survivor, it is not free from stereotyped passages. Seeck's judgment, on the other hand, "in der Darstellung der Kriegszüge und Schlachten strebt er mehr nach rhetorischem Prunk, als nach sachlicher Klahrheit" (*RE*, s.v. Ammianus, col. 1852), is too sweeping, and does not differentiate sufficiently between those parts of the *History* where Ammianus is writing from personal experience from those where he is not.

[43] xix.8.5.

[44] xviii.6.23.

[45] Otto Seeck, *Geschichte des Untergangs der antiken Welt* IV, p. 195: "So wunderlich das geschraubte Latein seines Werkes auch ist, durch die Feinheit seiner Charakteristiken und die wuchtige Dramatik der Erzählung erweist er sich selbst des Tacitus, den er fortgesetzt hat, nicht ganz unwürdig." He praises Ammianus' powers of characterization even more highly in *RE*, s.v. Ammianus, col. 1852. His allusion to Ammianus' Latin should be discounted in the light of what has been said about this question in the text.

[46] xxx.4.8–22.

[47] xv.7.7–10; xxvii.3.11–14.

[48] xxii.12.6–7; xxv.5.17.

[49] J. Bidez, *La Vie de l'empereur Julien* (Paris, 1930), p. 272.

[50] xxi.1.14.

[51] Ensslin, *op. cit.*, pp. 48 ff.

[52] Bidez, *op. cit.*, p. 337. I do not understand on what grounds Mr. Thompson (*Hermathena* 59, p. 46) asserts that since about 1887 "Ammianus' reputation as a historian has steadily declined." We have noted some adverse judgments in the text. Against these can be set the highly favorable opinions of Seeck, Mackail, Bidez, and the late Ernst Stein. The last-named even went so far (*Geschichte des spätrömischen Reiches*, p. 331) as to call Ammianus "das grösste literarische Genie . . . das die Welt unseres Erachtens zwischen Tacitus und Dante gesehen hat."

# INDEXES

# INDEX OF QUOTED ANCIENT AUTHORS

# GENERAL INDEX